STARTING SMALL-SCALE BUSINESS

"From Dreams to Dollars: A Beginner's Step-by-Step Guide to Business Success – Your Personal Blueprint for a Thriving Entrepreneurial Journey"

By

Arnette C. Briggs

Copyright

Disclaimer

The information handed in this book,"(Book Title)," is for general instructional purposes only. Every trouble has been made to insure that the content is accurate and over- to- date at the time of publication. still, the author makes no representation or guaranties of any kind, express or inferred, about the absoluteness, delicacy, trustability, felicity, or vacuity concerning the information, products, services, or affiliated plates contained in this book for any purpose. Any reliance you place on similar information is thus rigorously at your own threat. In no event will the author be liable for any loss or damage including without limitation, circular or consequential loss or damage, or any loss or damage whatsoever arising from the use of this book. The addition of links to third- party websites doesn't inescapably indicate a recommendation or plump the views expressed within them. Every trouble is made to keep the book over and running easily. still, the author takes no responsibility for, and won't be liable for, the book being temporarily unapproachable due to specialized issues beyond our control.

About the author

Allow me to introduce myself—I am Arnette C. Briggs the author of the book you've just delved into, " Starting small-scale business."

Writing this book has been a labor of love, born out of a passion for entrepreneurship and a desire to share valuable insights with fellow dreamers and doers.

In my journey through the realms of business, I've worn various hats—from startup enthusiast to seasoned entrepreneur. My experiences, both triumphs, and trials, have woven the fabric of this book. Every chapter is a reflection of lessons learned, challenges overcome, and a genuine belief in the transformative power of small-scale business.

Outside the world of words, My commitment to fostering growth, innovation, and resilience in the entrepreneurial community is not just a professional endeavor but a personal mission.

I believe that every small business has the potential to create a ripple effect, leaving an indelible mark on its community and the larger world. My hope is that this book serves as a guiding light, offering practical advice, inspiration, and a roadmap for those navigating the exhilarating yet challenging landscape of entrepreneurship.

As you turn the last page, I invite you to stay connected. Your stories, feedback, and shared experiences are what fuel the fire of my passion for this journey. Let's continue this dialogue, learn from each other, and celebrate the incredible ventures that sprout from the seeds of small-scale businesses.

Thank you for entrusting me with a part of your reading journey. May your entrepreneurial endeavors be filled with growth, fulfillment, and boundless success.

TABLE OF CONTENT

INTRODUCTION

Setting out on the excursion of beginning a limited scale business is much the same as sowing a seed with the possibility to develop into a thriving tree. In the domain of business, where dreams meet assurance, the choice to start a private venture addresses a significant obligation to individual and monetary development. Welcome to "Beginning Limited scope Business," an aide made to engage and move those at the edge of innovative investigation.

This book is intended for the visionaries, the visionaries, and the hard workers who imagine a reality molded by their interesting thoughts and tries. Whether you're venturing into the domain of independent work, developing a part time job, or sending off a private company with huge goals, this guide is custom fitted to go with you on your excursion.

With an emphasis on a fledgling cordial methodology, we explore through the complexities of business venture, separating complex ideas into reasonable advances. Every section unfurls useful models, giving unmistakable bits of knowledge and significant procedures to change your business desires into a reality.

In the pages that follow, you'll track down an abundance of data, from understanding the key standards of business to creating your customized plan for progress. We dive into monetary establishments, showcasing techniques, client associations, and the functional complexities that support a flourishing limited scope endeavor.

This book isn't simply a manual; it's a friend on your pioneering experience. It's here to be useful, to rouse, and to direct you through the interesting and, on occasion, testing landscape of beginning and growing a limited scale business. Thus, we should leave on this extraordinary excursion together, transforming your goals into accomplishments and your fantasies into a supportable reality.

Setting the Stage for a Transformative Journey

Drink to the morning of your adventure! Starting a small- scale business is like opening a door to endless possibilities, and this chapter is where we lay the root for the amazing trip ahead. Think of this chapter as the starting point of a discussion between musketeers. We will sputter about your dreams, what got you agitated about this adventure, and the unique vision you have for your business. Together, we'll uncover the passion that will drive your sweats and make your business trip not just about making a living but about living your dream. To navigate the entrepreneurial geography, we'll explore both your particular provocations and the broader trends in the request. Do not worry; we'll keep it light and pleasurable. It's about understanding where you fit into the big picture and what makes your business idea special. But hey, let's be real – starting a business is not always a walk in the demesne. That is why we'll talk about adaptability and the mindset that will help you bounce back from challenges. After all, lapses are just part of the trip, and with the right mindset, you can turn them into stepping monuments. Through some fun exercises and thoughtful reflections, you will start to see your business pretensions taking shape. By the end of this chapter, you will not only have a clearer picture of your path but also the excitement and confidence to take that first step. So, snare a mug of coffee or your favorite libation, get comfortable, and let's sputter about your dreams and the inconceivable trip you are about to embark on. It's time to set the stage for your small- scale business adventure! Whether you 're looking for a comprehensive business revamp or just seeking to take your company's operations to a new position, transubstantiating your business is a grueling , multifaceted trip that takes you into unknown terrain. exhaustively planning, preparing, and executing your transition in five distinct phases significantly increases your chance of success. utmost commercial leaders have come to realize that abecedarian business metamorphosis enterprise will be ineluctable as their companies are facing fleetly changing profitable and social surroundings. numerous of them will formerly have a clear understanding of the direction they must move in to ameliorate their business. The challenge, still, is in successfully orchestrating that change. As with other complex tasks, learning this challenge requires doing the right effects in the right order. Transformation peregrinations generally follow five distinct phases fantasize, explore, prepare, execute, andaccelerate.However, whereby all applicable aspects are considered and integrated in each step of the trip, following these phases will minimize your threat of failure, If conducted completely. fastening on certain areas of action while ignoring others isn't an effective game plan for success. It's necessary to unfold the contents of these five phases holistically to gradationally make up instigation, secure stakeholder commitment and support, and ramp- up your transition conditioning. In numerous ways, this is an iterative process that will include shifting back and forth between the phases to incorporate fresh perceptivity. But do n't be hysterical to pivot. Indeed, look forward to it.

1) Envision – defining the purpose of your metamorphosis Vision statements are used

to help enterprises communicate their abecedarian purpose and pretensions to stakeholders. By creating an charming image of an aspirational future, compelling vision statements inspire action and give guidance and direction. In the environment of metamorphosis, companies profit from developing and communicating a specific, change- related metamorphosis vision. Executing change in a commercial terrain generally induces a high degree of instability for numerous stakeholders. The better you can communicate the beginning purpose, pretensions, and benefits, the more buy- in and support for the change you'll get from all involved parties. styles and tools like Business Model Innovation and Value Proposition Design will help you develop a thorough and robust image of implicit unborn business. still, an effective metamorphosis vision not only depicts the target but also outlines the path forward. also, it communicates(maybe implicitly) the benefits to all involved parties, persuading them that it's worth the trouble and investment. thus, insure you have a clear, holistic vision of where you want to go, why this change is necessary, and what's in it for your stakeholders. Take the time to produce a comprehensive, focused vision for your unborn business, and believe it's possible. Confidence begets confidence.

2) Explore – laying out the metamorphosis strategy Once you know where you're headed, it's important to explore the structure blocks of your metamorphosis action. Consider all areas of action within the environment of their dynamic surroundings. also, uncover and estimate the collective interdependencies among the colorful structure blocks. For illustration, commercial leaders may ask themselves In which way do I need to change how our company addresses the requirements of guests? From that question, suppose a couple of way ahead What does this indicate in respects to the technology you use? Do you need to educate and enable your staff to work else? Do you have to acclimate your

organizational structures? These questions may feel egregious, but it's essential to fantasize these connections. else, some of these connections may be overlooked during medication and prosecution. Embarking on a metamorphosis trip generally means that you're planning for the long haul. When developing your metamorphosis strategy, it's also important to bear in mind that external developments continue to impact and impact your transition. New technologies may render your current approach to digital metamorphosis short- lived. Social developments(like the fall- eschewal from COVID- 19) can have vast impacts on hand geste

and prospects. And being challengers or recently- entering rivals may suddenly advance, leaving you in a mischievous competitive situation.

3) Prepare – evolving the metamorphosis approach and roadmap Strategy without prosecution is daydream. And prosecution without medication is hyperactivity. The

medication phase is the metamorphosis trip's crucial element that ensures that the asked changes are enforced effectively and efficiently — or not.

While the fantasize phase describes the " why " and the explore phase defines the " what, " the prepare phase elaborates on the " how. " It's in this stage that you unfold on which principles(organizational or methodological) you'll follow and which practices(Design Thinking, spare/ nimble) you plan to apply in each area of action. Then is, also, where you high the grounds for prosecution. Again, in order to insure a successful, end- to- end metamorphosis, the principles and practices applied in the colorful areas of action must be aligned and integrated. Experience shows that enterprise to apply new ways of working are bound to fail if they aren't exhaustively addressed. Ignoring certain aspects of a transition, similar as the people- side of change, can significantly harm the success of your action. Understanding the principles behind tools and practices enables you to more define the interfaces among different methodologies. This, in turn, will allow you to develop a sustainable roadmap for your metamorphosis trip.

4) Execute – integrating strategy with reality As soon as you 've concluded your medication and have defined your metamorphosis roadmap, you're ready to go. Now change operation will come the name of the game educating and enabling your association will be central to enforcing and administering the necessary changes. Proven methodologies like the Prosci ® ADKAR approach can be extremely precious in erecting the instigation and support needed on a stakeholder position. In substance, this is where superintendent graveness will make all the difference. By laboriously and visibly leading the change, top operation becomes the catalyst for success. leading metamorphosis enterprise with particular involvement, passion, and empathy holds

great influence and shows the genuine concern of commercial leadership.

5) Accelerate – reiterate, learn, pivot, and repeat So, you 've got your metamorphosis trip well- planned and successfully demurred- off? Good. Now make sure that you 're not losing ground or get wedged. ultramodern organizational models embrace change and account for it by enforcing nonstop check and acclimatize cycles. It's important that you aren't doing so on functional situations only. Set a visible illustration by transparently examining and conforming at the top position of operation. Make sure to regularly review all applicable areas of action and integrate the entire C-position leadership platoon in doing so. Assess the progress across the colorful structure blocks by agitating the following questions within your enterprise leadership circle Is your refurbished business model still doable? Are your strategic changes effective in reducing organizational waste? Is your technology mound state- of- the- art

and generating the value anticipated? Does your HR approach succeed in hiring the right people and developing the needed capacities and capabilities? And most importantly Does the integration of principles and practices insure that all applicable areas of action are addressed and developed exhaustively? If "yes" is the response to those queries, then great! Continue.However, reprise, If not. Navigating your metamorphosis trip with a structured, coordinated approach will help insure you and your business transition successfully. Our Transformation Board will work with you to exhaustively unfold on each phase of the metamorphosis trip by consolidating and imaging, and integrating the colorful areas of action with external influences. Designed as an easy- to-understand, easy- to- use conception, the Transformation Board will come your go- to tool to snappily and fluently insure you 're right on track.

CHAPTER 1

UNDERSTANDING BUSINESS BASICS

Learning business can be bogarting at the launch. With a wide range of specialized terms to be familiar with, and important generalities to understand. It really is no surprise that a good number of people believe learning business is relatively delicate. still, with the right mindset and amenability to learn, learning business can be delightful and easy to grasp. That's why this composition will be diving everything you should know about the basics of business.

Business basics

In business it's important to learn the basics of business before moving on to more sophisticated strategies. There are business basics that you need to be apprehensive of in order to come a successful, robust business for the long- term. In this composition you will learn about the foundational principles for business. You 'll also find out how you can apply them in your own assiduity.

Once you've got a strong foundation for your enterprise you will be more deposited for innovative thinking and be ready to come an assiduity leader. Innovation is vital for any launch- up because it allows you to find ways on how you can stand out from the competition. You need to be different and innovative in order for your business to thrive long- term.

The first step is understanding the basics of how you are going to run your company, which means making a solid plan that outlines all aspects of how you will operate.

This will help you avoid numerous miscalculations and insure that you have everything covered. The basics of business are the first way you should take in order to be successful. probing your guests and understanding their requirements and prospects will allow you to produce a sustainable business still you must first start with the introductory business chops needed.

Business chops

John Flow, an expert in company conformation, business critic, and proprietor ofLLC.services countries, that every entrepreneur should have practical thinking and be sufficiently flexible since these chops are the main and necessary for long- term business. This means that every entrepreneur should be equipped with chops that are essential for a long- continuing business. therefore, practical thinking serves an important part in choosing the right decision for any situation. Business openings do n't come veritably frequently. This is precisely why being a one- trick pony has no place in the business world.

Operation

Operation is a pivotal introductory skill for businesses. It's what allows you to prevision forthcoming situations and organize effects demanded. Without proper operation, everything additional falls because your business would have no direction. Accordingly, having no direction for your business plans will really affect in ruin, and you would n't like that. Good operation for small businesses can start with robotization similar as communication.

Business Fundamentals
Understanding The Basics Of Business

Managing a business does n't have to be delicate when you have a strategic plan laid out. You can delegate tasks to specific people. But insure that you only delegate tasks to able people. Doing so will help you guarantee the quality of the affair and optimize time. It's why you should be suitable to have a good relationship with your platoon and know them well, so you know whom to trust with vital effects for your success.

Practical thinking is important for every situation possible precisely because it allows you to be decisive in choosing the stylish course of action for the stylish outgrowth possible without a big threat of losing commodity. Surely, some opinions bear you to risk commodity. still, being practical allows you to decide intelligently while being calculated. For illustration, there are areas where it may make sense to pinch and cut gratuitous spendings, similar as extravagant entertainment or customer feasts, but others, similar as securing your demesne, where it surely would not.

One aspect of practical thinking is knowing when to cut corners dashingly without immolating your products and operations. Controllable charges are named as similar because you can eventually control them. And when you negotiate this, you'll be suitable to see an increase in your nethermost line or your profit.

Long- term thinking

For a good entrepreneur to be GREAT, long-term thinking is a skill that's surely demanded. As a business proprietor, you want to know what's a real necessity, and what's only trending at the present time. An intriguing illustration is how entrepreneurs frequently skip out on guarding their incipiency's intellectual property which more frequently than not, leads to theft or abuse of the same, therefore performing in the business getting destroyed. Choosing long- term opinions allows your business to grow indeed further and evolve through the times, and that's precisely what a good business demands for it to last long. incapability to choose opinions for long-term plans will risk consumers losing interest as item needs change.

Rigidity

Consideration for the client's changing requirements is commodity that every good business must keep in mind. However, also your company risks getting outdated and obsolete, If you aren't suitable to acclimatize. In recent times, numerous businesses have been forced to acclimatize due to extremity. For illustration, the manufacturing assiduity has faced global force chain challenges and some have chosen to pivot their businesses. This has helped them stay round for the short- term and conceivably come more robust and profitable for the long- term. Another great illustration is how elderly living installations like Vivante Living have acclimated to the COVID19 epidemic by chancing creative yet safe ways to help the residers stay active and engaged.

Introductory Strategy
Business openings bear on- point opinions, and on- point decision- making requires a practical approach. In some situations, entrepreneurs might indeed consider a

plutocrat lender loan to kickstart or Gauge their operations. introductory business strategy is essential for every starting entrepreneur anyhow of the type of business they are trying to commit to- whether it's a traditional slipup- and- mortar store or a more contemporary and accessible online business. It allows you to suppose completely before any action and act according to any situation. Your business must have both strategic and practical thinking in order to develop, endure, and thrive. also, strategic planning can win hearts and minds of the platoon you'll make. The platoon will have further trust in the leadership if they know that people who maneuver the company make intelligent opinions for their long- term stability.

Learn your request.
It's essential to learn your request. It allows you to be knowledgeable about what your target request is in need of. With this, having full knowledge of what your target request wants gives you all the information you

need to acclimate what's demanded for your product or service. Without the understanding of what your target request requirements, you would not be suitable to bring out the stylish in your products or services that your guests are looking for. You need to be suitable to break the problems of your target request. Their life should be made as straightforward and doable as possible by your products.

When you can identify this, you can produce further products aligned with your objects, therefore expanding your product line and brand integrity.

Quality over volume

Quality is one of the most important effects when it comes to the basics of business. guests will choose quality over volume 10 times out of ten. It's important to insure that your products or services are top quality. This will also leave your guests wanting more. fastening on the thickness of quality rather than volume holds great significance, particularly on the life of your product and how well it's made.

Likewise, the quality of your product can be your sole marketing strategy because a great product will do its job of spreading positive words to others through feedback, witnesses, and positive reviews, similar as CherryPicks. When it comes to services, excellent worker performance is necessary for a quality service.

And excellent training with your platoon fastening on the significance of client experience should be a top precedence. Your entire pool should be your brand ministers every time they wear your totem or hallmark, especially outside work.

Social media and online marketing

Social media and online selling give a huge occasion for businesses, especially starting businesses. This is primarily because the ultramodern world is more dependent on the use of the internet to browse about particular requirements and wants. Marketing through online advertisements or websites will really attract your guests. Especially, as your products or services produce an enticing impact once they see that it's indeed top quality.

Apps are another means of growing your business and structurecommunity.However, it builds community and gives you a close-knit followership and way to interact with your guests to make fidelity, grow deals, If you have a great interactive app. Indeed free apps can help. You may ask," how do free apps make plutocrat?" and the response is that they can do so through marketing, upsells, and other means.

Bodying the client experience goes a long way to creating repeat guests. These guests will give you their business over and over and over again. You can use the online folder maker to produce digital marketing accoutrements similar as leaflets, registers, or eBooks with a smooth runner- flipping effect that resembles a real publication. also you can partake it via dispatch or on your social media biographies to make brand mindfulness and request your products. Brands generally use digital marketing to increase brand recognition and establish a presence in their assiduity. A large chance of the world's population is online. Reaching out to them has come flawless with a many gates of your cutlet. You need to use this medium effectively to make your business prosper. Basics Of Business Business ethics and force One of the most important basics of business is the proper care for your workers. Guidance and watch for force must be a precedence above all, as everyone has equal rights. This means furnishing the stylish plant for your pool to motivate them and insure they're comfortable. icing your workers are fit and healthy also helps to boost their morale. With an encouraging terrain and a group of fit individualities, it's without a mistrustfulness that your business will grow further. Monitoring their metabolism can assist them in maintaining their health.

10 basics of business

Then are 10 business basics you can source when trying to ameliorate business processes

1. Marketing and imprinting Understanding marketing and branding processes can be salutary to developing an effective client base. Both departments are pivotal factors that educate people about a business and convert them to buy products or services. One of the most effective ways to understand marketing is to learn the way in a client's decision- making process and how those way relate to introductory marketing ways. You can also develop your own marketing ways by targeting certain way.

2. fiscal operation It's frequently essential for companies to understand how to manage business finances. In the early stages of a business, a large part of this operation entails attaining incipiency costs. Whether it's through a loan, crowdfunding, subventions, investors or an proprietor's plutocrat, it's important for prospective possessors to maintain detailed records of how they attained their backing. It's also

important to have a strategy for how to use the attained finances and develop cash inflow prognostications.

3. Accounting Accounting differs slightly from fiscal operation because it focuses more on regular charges and income involved with a business. Learning the fundamentals of account entails learning about the records businesses need to maintain and how to keepthem.However, they may be suitable to negotiate this kind of account with a introductory spreadsheet and a system for organizing bills and other forms, If an proprietor operates a small business. It may also be helpful to exploration account software for small businesses. Larger companies frequently employ entire account departments.

4. Strategic operation It's important for companies to have and execute a business strategy. In the early stages of a company, this largely entails creating a business plan, which generally contains business pretensions and plans for achieving them. Strategic operation remains important

through all stages of a business, as it also involves streamlining pretensions and perfecting the plans for meeting those pretensions. Related Strategic Planvs. Business Plan What is the Difference?

5. Research and development numerous products or services bear exploration and development both before and after their creation. Before you begin dealing a product or service, this process may include probing its request and competition and developing your particular interpretation. It's important to continue conducting exploration so you can find new ways to ameliorate your product and remain competitive. Understanding how exploration and development work can be vital for anyone wanting to insure success within their business. 6. People operation A vital aspect of operating a successful business is being suitable to manage workers. Whether running a small business with a many workers or managing 50 people, people operation can help insure effective directorial ways. A business has a better

chance of success when the people who work there can communicate effectively, understand their liabilities, have the tools they need to succeed and feel inspired to achieve their pretensions. It's frequently essential to learn how to produce a healthy, encouraging work terrain that allows workers to be productive and pious. Affiliated companion to People Management Definition, Tips and Chops

7. Legal aspects Comprehending the legal implications of a certain enterprise is also crucial. This can include deciding on the applicable legal business structure, pursuing necessary licenses and clinging to applicable regulations. It can also include understanding contracts you might enter, similar as bones

with workers, merchandisers or freelancers. Consider learning about applicable business lawfulness by consulting with a counsel, talking to someone with experience in your business area or conducting your own exploration.

8. seller operation still, it's important to understand how to work with them, If your business collaborates with external merchandisers. External merchandisers may include a ranch that supplies constituents for a eatery, a printing service that creates business cards, letterhead and leaflets or a courier service that vessels products. occasionally, you might use an external seller only formerly for a special occasion, but others you might use further regularly. Consider learning about how to choose a seller, associated costs, implicit contract terms and how to make a successful long-term relationship with merchandisers. Affiliated What Is Vendor Management and How To Conduct It(With Tips)

9. Negotiating Negotiating can be an important skill for numerous business situations. For illustration, you might negotiate with a seller for a deal on bulk purchases or develop a contract with a freelancer. Some small businesses negotiate trades on services, similar as a small catering business supplying a marketing

business with feeding for a work event in exchange for marketing services. Being suitable to negotiate effectively can help insure an outgrowth that is fair and salutary for all parties involved.

10. Networking Networking can be a salutary skill to retain in the business assiduity. By learning how to network in your assiduity or with other business professionals, you can find numerous openings to ameliorate a business. For illustration, networking can lead to your connections recommending your product or services to new guests and guests. It may also lead to openings to work with new merchandisers, attend events and meet more educated professionals who can advise you.

Navigating the Fundamentals with a Beginner-Friendly Approach

Okay, how about we plunge into the bare essential of beginning your limited scale business, yet relax I am then to direct you through everything in the most amicable manner conceivable. Consider this section your compass through the rudiments, planned in light of apprentices. Beginning with the basics of entrepreneurship, we'll break down complicated terms and ideas into manageable gobbets. No demand for extravagant language then; We're remaining straightforward and straightforward. From understanding your request to sorting out your intriguing selling suggestion, we've you covered. Have you ever felt lost among the ROI, KPI, or P&L acronyms? Be at ease! We will clarify the financial side of effects similar that indeed the individualities who are not figures individualities can appreciate. You will explore financial records like an ace when we are finished. still, it goes beyond proposition Practicality will be incorporated into each step. suppose of this chapter as a hands- on factory where you learn the fundamentals and put them to use in your own business idea. It's like having a trainer right there with you, guiding you and encouraging you. We will probe the basics of planning and financial medication, icing you have a strong root to expand upon. It's like making a road chart for your business that will help you confidently navigate the twists and turns. As we sail through this part, we'll examine the force of feasible correspondence in business. From creating your image communication to uniting with your ideal interest group, you will ahead long be a maestro in conveying your business story. What is further, hello, promoting does not need to be an inviting word. We will disentangle the secrets of showcasing methodologies, zeroing in on approaches that work for private companies. Picture this as your promoting tool store, loaded up with useful hints and deceives to make your business hang out in a packed marketable center. Toward the finish of this part, you will get a handle on the rudiments of business as well as sense engaged to apply them to your one of a kind circumstance. So, buckle up for a fun and instructional trip through the fundamentals in which literacy is delightful and the trip is just as important as the destination. Together, we'll explore the enterprising abysses and make the rudiments work for you.

Clearly! Let's break down the meanings of these acronyms

1. ROI Return on Investment Meaning ROI is a fiscal standard used to estimate the profitability of an investment. It's calculated by dividing the net gain from the investment by the original cost of the investment. The result is generally expressed as a chance. A positive ROI indicates a profitable investment, while a negative ROI suggests a loss.

2. KPIs crucial Performance pointers Meaning KPIs are quantifiable criteria used to measure the performance of a business or a specific aspect of it. They help associations track progress toward pretensions and objects. KPIs can vary depending on the nature of the business but frequently include criteria related to deals, client satisfaction, hand performance, and more.

3. P&L Profit and Loss Meaning P&L, also known as an income statement, is a fiscal statement that summarizes the earnings, costs, and charges incurred during a specific

period(generally a financial quarter or time). It shows whether a company is making a profit or passing a loss by abating total charges from total profit. The nethermost line of the statement reflects the net profit or net loss. Understanding these acronyms is pivotal for assessing the fiscal health and performance of a business. They give precious perceptivity for decision-timber, strategy development, and overall operation of a company. directors and other business professionals may use colorful tools in order to produce an effective and productive work terrain. One fashion is to produce a list of abecedarian business principles in order to outline the company's core values and prospects. Understanding what these principles are can help you determine whether you'd like to apply this practice within your business.

What are abecedarian business principles?
Abecedarian business principles are statements that a company or association adheres to in order to identify its

precedences and companion future opinions. These principles may address effects like association and strategy or client experience and satisfaction. They may also be specific to a platoon or company and take over specific pretensions or assiduity- related operations. A pot may publish its abecedarian business principles for its consumers to read, or a platoon may publish theirs for other workers to view.

10 abecedarian business principles Then is a list of 10 abecedarian business principles to consider

1. Know the assiduity and your challengers Assiduity knowledge can be an important aspect of business leadership and may impact your norms of business operation and strategy. Consider probing the request you are in or uniting with assiduity experts in order to ameliorate your understanding of what consumers anticipate and watch about. also, learning about your challengers' pricing, quality and marketing strategies can

help insure that you are offering guests a product that's applicable and adequately priced. This information can help you stand out amongst analogous businesses and appeal to the customer in a unique way.

2. make a good platoon This abecedarian business principle can be salutary for numerous work surroundings, anyhow of your assiduity. Having platoon members that are enthusiastic and well- trained can help insure that your business strategies and operations are successful. Competent workers can bring innovative ideas or applicable assiduity knowledge to your company and continually ameliorate the quality and delivery of your products. Feting your platoon's chops and accomplishments can encourage them to continue to perform their stylish, so training them to do their stylish can have positive goods on the company and workers overall.

3. produce a high- quality product Creating a high- quality product can set your company

piecemeal from challengers and motivate guests to be pious to your brand. Successful companies may generally produce well-made products or services that address the preferences and solicitations of the consumer. fastening on the quality of your wares can ameliorate client satisfaction by furnishing them with positive and harmonious relations with your brand. This may help grow your customer base and brand mindfulness.

4. Define your pretensions It's generally a good idea to define your pretensions and business objects, making this a precious abecedarian principle. Creating pretensions can help you track your success and progress, and identify when to award workers for theirefforts.However, a list of objects can be a helpful tool, If you are determined on growing your business or consumer base. Consider creating a plan or figure for how to achieve each thing, and consult with other platoon members to

assemble a manageable list of effective tasks.

5. Promote your products or services
Another abecedarian business principle is to promote your product or services. professed deals and advertising ways can ameliorate your profit and profit and contribute to your company's success. Consider making a deals plan and a marketing plan in order to have an effective and sustainable approach. workers can use a deals plan to promote specific products for a designated quantum of time in order to yield an ideal quantum of profit. Alternately, a marking plan grows brand mindfulness within your assiduity overall and is less focused on specific quantifiable measures.

6. Understand organizational structure
Understanding how successful businesses leaders organize and operate their companies can help you apply analogous strategies within your own association. There are numerous aspects of structure within a

business, including the operation of systems, the allocation of tasks and the composition of labor force or workers within a department. learning effective business structures can help you insure that your company is remaining as productive and effective as possible.

7. Know the principles of finance and account In addition to company structures, understanding crucial information related to finance and account may be a abecedarian business principle. This can guarantee that your association continuously adheres to the laws and regulations of your assiduity. Finance and counting information may include the necessary levies to fill out, permits to apply for and deadlines to meet. Some specific account principles include addendum principle thickness principle Full exposure principle profitable reality principle Matching principle traditionalism principle

8. Understand functional systems and processes Understanding functional systems and processes can be a precious business principle if you are trying to grow or gauge up the size and reach of your business. There are several functional systems you can consider, including Managing your guests Communicating with your platoon and guests Tracking your deals and marketing ways Supervising the spread of information through your company Keeping track of your deals and profit Affiliated The 5- Step Strategic Management Process

9. Use capital strategically The strategic use of your profit can be an integral aspect of your business's success. icing that you have sufficient finances to pay all of your workers and lot enough for fresh costs that may arise can allow you to continue to operate and grow your company. Knowing how to allocate your gains can make it possible to continue to produce and ameliorate upon your products and wares.

10. Prioritize your guests It can be salutary for your association to prioritize your guests and give them with products that address their interests and solicitations. You can concentrate on client service to insure they feel like you watch about their issues and enterprises. It may be easier to vend a new product or upsell being products to an established client than to find new guests, so it's salutary for your brand to maintain positive connections with them so that they continue to buy or consume your goods and services.

Benefits of abecedarian business principles
Abecedarian business principles can have numerous benefits for your company and help you establish and maintain successful practices. These principles can profit businesses in the following ways:

Creating a foundation They can help produce a foundation on which all company stakeholders make trust and form professional connections. These stakeholders can include guests, shareholders, workers and suppliers.

Guiding decision- making: A list of applicable principles can give operation with guidance in decision- making situations. This list can also help them produce strategic plans and navigate what their platoon can do in order to negotiate given tasks.

Establishing a company culture: By easily outlining the abecedarian business principles of your company, you can inform all workers and stakeholders regarding the prospects, values and norms you intend to uphold. This can produce a distinct and established company culture where workers know how to succeed.

Distinguishing your company's unique identity: While there are general business principles that can apply to colorful companies and diligence, relating a specific list of what is important to you and your business can help distinguish its identity and set yourself piecemeal from challengers in your field.

Perfecting hand retention: By establishing a list of values and norms that align with your company, you can attract workers that agree with your vision and have a desire to join your platoon. This means that you may ameliorate your retention rates because workers know the prospects ahead of time and believe in your company's charge.

Swaying staff geste
 and practices Having an figure of the core principles of the company may impact the way workers bear and how they approach their jobduties.However, they may feel inclined to follow through with this practice, If they know the company as a whole prioritizes client satisfaction.

CHAPTER 2

CULTIVATING AN ENTREPRENEURIAL MINDSET

Entrepreneurs help bolster profitable development, produce jobs, and construct products or services that can make the world a better place. A good entrepreneur needs to think creatively and have big, audacious ideas. Anyone can come up with a new idea, but erecting a successful business around it's the entrepreneurial challenge. The entrepreneurial mindset is unique in that bone must be creative, communicative, and largely motivated to succeed, yet open to threat and failure.

A great idea by itself does not create a route to the pinnacle of achievement in entrepreneurship. hourly the success or failure of a business comes down to the characteristics of the entrepreneur themselves. It takes a unique total of characteristics to immingle one big idea into a completely-functional thriving business. Is there a certain blend of chops and traits which allows some entrepreneurs to come hectically successful?

Serve it to say that there's no magical formula to succeed in business(if so, Harvard Business School would have patented it). still, there are certain characteristics which all aspiring entrepreneurs should cultivate to dramatically boost their own odds for success. An entrepreneurial mindset, if you will, may mark the difference between a economic business and one which shutters the doors before the first time is over.

So what ARE these each-important characteristics aspiring or new entrepreneurs should cultivate? What attributes tend to cock the scales in favor of heading up a booming business?

1. A Positive Mental station Entrepreneurial Mindset

WHY IS A POSITIVE STATION IMPORTANT FOR ENTREPRENEURS?

A positive station and outlook is a must-have for successful entrepreneurs. The mindset of the head of the company sets the tone for the rest of the company and influences commercial culture.

Negative studies undermine forward stir and the progress of the company, not to mention the operation's capability to lead staff and motivate workers. Part of what gives entrepreneurs the fiber to rainfall the business downturns is positivity.

" When everything seems to be going against you, flash back that the aeroplane takes off in opposition to the wind, not toward it.

" – Henry Ford, author of Ford Motor Company.

Cultivating a positive station isn't about sticking your head in the beach and ignoring effects that could go awry, but about learning how to mentally reframe your response. There's no point in wallowing in miscalculations.

One way to change your outlook is to look a negative pain point and ask " How can I laboriously correct this? " You may easily learn how to cultivate a positive mindset toward change by examining how you respond to imagined problems.

Positive people look to challenges as a way to ameliorate and learn, so you should try to concentrate on this skill.

Why is positivity important for the overall work terrain? When you 're the master, a positive station influences others in a also positive way. exploration indicates that happy workers are better overall workers. Cerebral exploration has made a correlation between advanced productivity and positive work surroundings. also, positive work surroundings have been linked to advanced business gains, smaller sick days, and advanced staff retention rates. Indeed small changes can boost positivity. Visit our resource How to produce a Positive Work terrain to learn how to boost positivity in your company.

HOW CAN YOU CULTIVATE A POSITIVE STATION FOR BUSINESS?

Part of relinquishing negativity is realizing that your own negative studies as a company leader waste energy, time, and plutocrat.

Being positive is commodity which, like all life chops, can be learned. getting an entrepreneur isn't for the faint- hearted. The long hours and erratic demands of heading up your own company can negatively impact both your particular life and internal outlook.

One of the easiest ways to cultivate a positive station is to concentrate on the effects you can control. You can control your diet, quantum of sleep and capability to exercise. You'll remain optimistic, healthy, and focused with the support of each of these elements.

Where to find the time to make time for yourself when you 're working around the timepiece? Research has shown that indeed one ten- nanosecond walk each day can boost your mood and reduce rates of negative studies.

2. A Creative Mindset Entrepreneural Mindset
WHY IS A CREATIVE MINDSET IMPORTANT FOR ENTREPRENEURS? noway has the word " Creativity is the mama of invention " been nay than in the world of entrepreneurship. suppose of Steve Jobs and the iPhone. Edison and the light bulb. The Wright Sisters and the aeroplane.

Each of these ground- breaking inventions would not have come to consummation were it not for healthy boluses of creative discretion.

Indeed if you 're not in a " creative " assiduity, creativity is demanded for entrepreneurial success. The mind of an entrepreneur is always looking for new ideas and inventions. The introductory life cycle of any entrepreneurial product stems from the generality of an idea followed by turning that idea into a feasible product or service.

" Creativity is just connecting goods. When you ask creative people how they did commodity, they feel a little shamed because they did n't really do it, they just saw commodity. It sounded obvious to them after a while. That's because they were suitable to connect exploits they 've had and synthesize new goods. - Steve Jobs Being the master allows you to express your creative every single day, which is one of its numerous advantages. You get to test out innovative strategies to ameliorate and modify your business. Indeed if you 're not in a creative field, per se, working out ways to optimize your business operations is a creative act. When you 're heading up your own company, you can apply creative thinking to your deals, PR, hiring, tech the list is endless.

CULTIVATING A INSPIRING intelligence IN BUSINESS WHAT IS IT? utmost entrepreneurs are constitutionally creative thinkers; differently, they would not be inspired to take the innovative vault to produce their own business. That said, we can all learn to be more creative and to stopcock into our essential bents. Whether or not you believe that creativity is blessed to some or a learned particularity, there are ways to learn to cultivate your creative mind. Visit Entrepreneur's 5 Brain Training ways to Your Creative Genius to learn how to cultivate and tap into your own creative mind.

3. Conclusive Communication Capability Entrepreneurial Mindset

WHY IS PERSUASIVENESS IMPORTANT FOR ENTREPRENEURS? The swish entrepreneurs are conclusive individualities. The power of persuasion can help you negotiate, close a trade, or score a lower price on your force. Not to mention, conclusive people tend to be inspiring leaders, ergo they tend to be astral heads.

Still, you must appeal to interest rather than intellect, " If you would convert. " – Benjamin Franklin

CULTIVATING A INSPIRING MENTALITY IN BUSINESS WHAT IS IT? While some people are more naturally conclusive than others, conclusive communication chops can be learned and rehearsed. Learning to communicate and present your ideas will make you a better entrepreneur — no matter what your sedulity is. learning conclusive tactics can mean the difference between financial success or ruin. also's how to make the art of persuasion work for you in business.

REPAY

Cerebral disquisition has shown the " reciprocity rule " can be truly effective in business. The basics of the rule in plain language is that when a person does you a favor, you must give a favor in return. Try to make your conclusive case by " giving " commodity to the person you 're trying to convert. You may just close the deal or make the trade.

LOOK TO OTHERS

Social substantiation is the generality that people look to others for how to bear in social settings. Social substantiation can be used as a conclusive toolinbusiness.However, showing how the product has been successful for others can help make that trade, If you 're trying to sell one of your products.

USE LABELS

Appealing to one's character is a important conclusive tool. You can use this mode of persuasion by indicating that they should act in a way which is harmonious with a marker. For illustration, say, " Your café is a fine French café and good French caffs stock our wine. " This is a common tactic used in marketing campaigns to make deals.

4. Natural Provocation and Drive Entrepreneurial Mindset

WHY IS NATURAL PROVOCATION IMPORTANT FOR ENTREPRENEURS?

One of the top entrepreneurial characteristics is natural provocation, meaning you are tone- motivated as opposed to looking to others to push you to do goods or hold you responsible. vastly speaking, those who enjoy their own businesses are incredibly motivated to succeed. They 've poured blood, sweat, and rips into their company, and may have literally pledged their future to first open their businesses ' doors. Having a lot at stake tête- à- tête powers the motivational drive.

" The secret of change is to concentrate all your energy not on fighting the old but on erecting the new. - Socratic

CAN NATURE PROVOCATION BE CULTIVATED FOR BUSINESS?

Prosperous business possessors understand that maintaining provocation is essential to operating a profitable enterprise. What way can you take to cultivate this provocation?

One way to stay motivated in the long- term is to keep the focus on the endgame, the big picture. Where is your company headed? What plans do you have in the future to grow and expand? How will your company fit into its separate sedulity in the future? Experts say that formulating long- range pretensions and plans keeps the motivational fires burning.

Speaking of thing setting, experts also advise that thing setting is another way to keep your motivational machine turning.

The key to using pretensions for provocation is to set high- quality pretensions.

What does that mean? basically, high-quality pretensions are clear, attainable, and manageable. As an illustration," This month, I will be attending two continuing education courses." Or " I will hire an editor for my company website by Friday. " High- quality pretensions give a sense of provocation when you negotiate your intended ideal. When you 're the master, you 're not only responsible for your own natural provocation, but you 're also responsible for cultivating that for your workers.

5. Tenacity and an Capability to Learn from Failure Entrepreneurial Mindset

WHY IS LITERACY FROM IMPORTANT FOR ENTREPRENEURS?

When you launch a business, your dream is to make it extremely successful. It's true that success is awful, but failure is where growth and change be. The crucial to learning from failure is miscalculation so actually learn and embrace your miscalculations so they make your better, not break you.

" Every failure is a step to success. - Malcolm Forbes

Avoid being too eager to fail, as you'll be with like-minded individuals whenever you do. The richest business possessors, utmost decorated sports stars, and well- known artists have all failed at one time or another in their path to riches and fame. Everyone is mortal, thus, amiss. Don't anticipate yourself to be perfect in the pursuit of your business dream. It is, by description, insolvable.

IN BUSINESS, HOW CAN YOU CULTURATE RESILIENCE & TAKE IN PROGRESS FROM BEING UNSUCCESSFUL?

Failure is ineluctable, but your response to your failure is what you make of it. Then's how to cultivate that and use your failure to come out indeed more successful in long-term.

DO N'T BE SHAMED OF YOUR REVERSAL

Don't attach judgment or blame when you fail. Business failure shouldn't make you feel shamed or embarrassed. Do your stylish to remove the emotion from miscalculations you make as an entrepreneur so you can logically explore how to better yourself and your company. Turn off your negative tone-talk and learn to say " Now I know more for coming time! " rather.

USE TOUGH TIMES TO LEARN FROM ADVERSITY

Let times of adversity lead you to strength. Failure can be your stylish chance to learn how to do commodity right. As a launch- up new business proprietor and entrepreneur, you 're going to face numerous firsts — first customer, first business parcel, first hand hire. Some of these firsts are bound to not work out; that's okay and anticipated. Use these lapses to develop ideas and tactics for how you want to run your business in the future.

SHARE YOUR GESTS WITH OTHERS

Failing at commodity is mortal, which means that others have forged that path before you. Partake your gests with others you trust, whether it's your tutor, associates, or staff — to gain some outside perspective. participating that experience can help you unite to reach an indeed better result for how to handle a tricky problem in the future.

DON'T BE HYSTERICAL TO CHANGE COURSE AND RESET

Indeed the best- laid plans will occasionally go amiss. That's just how life and business work.

There will come a time when you may realize that commodity simply isn't working. You may have to acclimate your planned course, reset, and start over.

NOWAY GIVE UP!

One of the most important keys to success in entrepreneurship is to noway give up. You can conquer difficult situations with determination.

Be tenacious about working toward your dreams. With determination and fortitude, you 'll achieve them; it just may not be overnight!

Unleashing Inspiration for Your Entrepreneurial Spirit

Attending a recent conference, I had the honor of harkening to Jordan Belfort, the fabulous entrepreneur and motivational speaker, as he participated his profound perceptivity on colorful aspects of entrepreneurship, marketing, and deals. He's well known from the movie, The Wolf of Wall Street, and has come a sought- after deals leader and coach. Throughout his witching

talk, Belfort exfoliate light on the factors that hamper entrepreneurial success, the true substance of being an entrepreneur, the significance of provocation and deals training, and the vital part of spanning a business. In this comprehensive blog composition, we will claw into the crucial takeaways from his speech, exploring the inestimable assignments he communicated.

Understanding Entrepreneurship and the Value Proposition

Jordan Belfort began his talk by emphasizing that entrepreneurship goes beyond simply having a product or service; it's about casting a compelling value proposition. The key lies in effectively communicating this proposition to implicit guests. How an entrepreneur presents the value proposition can significantly impact the company's products and services perceived worth – it can either multiply or dwindle the value.

Learning From Failure Several times in the speech he participated stories about the failures he'd in business. One of his first business gambles, dealing firmed meat out of a truck, he grew too snappily and was n't capitalized duly. His ambition to grow outpaced his capability to sustain the growth, and the business failed. When he first got into his brokerage business, his deals ways failed miserably. He wasn't suitable to train his deals platoon or grow his company. When he was about to quit, he came up with the brilliant idea of the straight- line deals system. The low points in his career, whether business failure or going to captivity, he learned from his miscalculations and fully changed himself.

The crossroad of Marketing and Deals For an entrepreneur, the ultimate thing of marketing is to identify the stylish guests and bring them into the deals channel in a cost-effective manner. Belfort likened marketing to gasoline that energies the machine(deals). When selling sweats fall suddenly, it negatively affects the performance of the deals platoon, leading to an overzealous pursuit of leads to close deals. This also turns to a downcast curl of low morale among the deals platoon, lowered returns on current leads, and turning off the business to the company.

Nurturing Long- term provocation Keeping the deals platoon motivated in the long run is pivotal for sustained success. Belfort conceded that managing a small group of salesmen can be more grueling than handling a larger platoon. He emphasized the significance of the deals platoon's inner world, which encompasses maintaining a positive emotional state, cultivating empowering beliefs, and having a clear vision of both short- term and long- term pretensions.

Belfort encouraged salesmen to produce a vision board to fantasize their bournes easily. Aligning particular norms with this vision is essential; else, individualities may come either romanticists with high bournes but low norms or frustrated individualities with high norms but limited vision. True success lies in the consonance between vision and norms, performing in a important driving force for progress.

Significance of Delivering Value and Effective Deals Training

In the pursuit of entrepreneurial success, Belfort underscored the critical aspect of delivering value. Contrary to the misconception that businesses are solely about making plutocrat, he emphasized that furnishing value in a cost-effective manner is the foundation for sustainable gains.

Also, Belfort stressed that provocation without proper chops training is futile. To achieve excellence in deals, he prompted entrepreneurs to combine provocation with effective chops training. He introduced the " Straight Line Deals System, " which revolves around erecting trust and connections with guests, the deals platoon, and the company before making the final trade. This approach ensures that the deals process is flawless and client- acquainted, leading to advanced conversion rates and client satisfaction.

Learning the external World The Deals Process

Belfort stressed that every trade follows a analogous process. He described the " Straight Line Deals System " as a three- step approach that aligns the three core rudiments to a perfect ten before asking for the trade:

Move the Value Proposition: The first trade involves elevating the value proposition of the product or service from a one to a ten. By effectively explaining the value, the salesman can capture the interest and trust of implicit guests.

Sell Yourself: The alternate trade revolves around persuading the client that the salesman is secure, dependable, and authentically interested in meeting their requirements.

Vend the Company: The third trade focuses on establishing the company's character and credibility in the eyes of the client. When all three deals align, the deals process becomes smoother, and expostulations are addressed more effectively.

Handling Expostulations

Belfort explained that expostulations from implicit guests are frequently bomb defenses for query. rather of directly venting their lack of trust or product dissatisfaction, guests may present expostulations. Deals professionals must empathize with the client's enterprises and address them with tolerance and understanding. This approach builds trust and credibility, leading to increased chances of closing the trade. He also emphasized that in utmost businesses, there are generally veritably many expostulations. salesmen should be professed at responding to expostulations and leading them back along the straight line. generally, an expostulation is lack of trust for the product, salesman, or the company. relating the core reason for the expostulation will allow the salesman to " resell " the prospect on the correct area of concern.

The Art of Spanning a Business

As an entrepreneur's adventure grows, Belfort underlined the need to delegate liabilities and hire great people to grease expansion beyond a certain threshold. spanning a business from a small enterprise to a substantial company requires a different skill set and mind set, making it vital to acclimatize and evolve along the entrepreneurial trip.

Power of Scripts, part- playing

Belfort spoke passionately about the part of scripts in deals. Contrary to common misconceptions, he emphasized that scripts are essential tools that should noway be delivered as robotic harangues. duly trained deals professionals, through part- playing exercises and script mastery, can deliver important and conclusive deals pitches that connect with implicit guests on a deeper position.

CHAPTER 3

CRAFTING YOUR BUSI NESS BLUEPRINT

In moment's presto- paced and competitive business geography, having a solid business plan is more critical than ever. It's not just about having an idea or product to vend; it's about having a clear strategy, measurable objects, and a roadmap to achieve them. Your business plan is your company's foundation, guiding you through each step, helping you identify and avoid implicit pitfalls and obstacles, and icing you stay on track toward your pretensions.

Still, creating a business plan isn't just about writing a document; it's about assaying your business idea, understanding your target request, and developing a strategy that fits your unique vision and pretensions. It requires careful exploration, critical thinking, and strategic planning.

To help you produce a winning business plan,
I have collected a list of 10 stylish practices that successful business possessors and entrepreneurs use. Following these stylish practices can make a solid foundation for your business and insure its long- term success.

What's a business plan?
A business plan is a comprehensive document that outlines a company's strategy, pretensions, and fiscal protrusions. It provides a roadmap for the business and serves as a tool for decision- timber, fundraising, and communicating with stakeholders.

Stylish practices for creating a business plan
Easily define your business idea and objects
Your business plan should begin by easily explaining your vision, the problem it

solves, and the target request. Next, define your objects, including short- term and long-term pretensions.

Illustration: A incipiency that provides healthy, factory- grounded mess delivery services may define its ideal as furnishing accessible and affordable healthy mess options for busy professionals.
Conduct request exploration: Conduct thorough exploration to understand your target request, challengers, and assiduity trends. This will help you develop a unique value proposition and identify implicit challenges and openings.

Example: The healthy mess delivery incipiency may conduct request exploration to determine the demand for their services, identify their target request, and dissect the pricing and services offered by challengers.

Develop a marketing and deals strategy: Your business plan should include a detailed marketing and deals strategy that outlines how you'll reach and engage with your target request and convert them into guests.

Example: The healthy mess delivery incipiency may develop a marketing and deals strategy that includes social media advertising, influencer hookups, and dispatch marketing juggernauts.

Produce a fiscal plan: Develop a comprehensive fiscal plan that includes profit protrusions, charges, and cash inflow. This will help you determine the profitable feasibility of your business and secure backing.

Example: The healthy mess delivery incipiency may produce a fiscal plan that includes profit protrusions grounded on pricing, estimated charges for constituents, labor, and marketing, and a cash inflow analysis.

figure functional and operation structures: Your business plan should include details on the organizational structure, staffing requirements, and operating procedures. This will help you manage coffers effectively and insure the smooth operation of your business.

Example: The healthy mess delivery incipiency may outline its functional and operation structures, including the places and liabilities of staff, delivery procedures, and food medication protocols.

Include a Threat analysis: Identify implicit pitfalls and challenges impacting your business and develop contingency plans to alleviate them.

Example: The healthy mess delivery incipiency may identify implicit pitfalls, similar as force chain dislocations, food safety issues, and changes in consumer preferences, and develop contingency plans to address them.

Set measurable criteria: Your business plan should include quantifiable criteria to track progress toward your objects and acclimate strategies as demanded.

Example: The healthy mess delivery incipiency may set criteria similar as client accession cost, client retention rate, and profit growth to measure their progress toward their objects.

Keep it terse: Your business plan should be brief and fluently understood. Focus on the crucial rudiments and avoid gratuitous details.

Example: The healthy mess delivery incipiency may keep its business plan terse by using pellet points and visual aids to present information easily and compactly.

Get feedback: Partake your business plan with trusted counsels, instructors, and associates to get feedback and upgrade your strategies.

Example The healthy mess delivery incipiency may partake its business plan with assiduity experts, investors, and implicit mates to get feedback and perceptivity. Update regularly: Your business plan is a living document that should be streamlined regularly to reflect changes in your business, assiduity trends, and request conditions.

Example: The healthy mess delivery incipiency may modernize its business plan daily or annually to reflect changes in its pricing strategy, marketing channels, and client accession sweats.

Why is it vital to understand how to produce a business plan?

For a number of reasons, writing a business strategy is essential. First, it provides a clear roadmap for your business and helps you identify implicit

Openings and challenges. A well- drafted business plan can also help secure backing from investors or fiscal institutions. Eventually, regularly streamlining your business plan can help you stay on track and acclimate your strategies as demanded.

In addition, a well- drafted business plan is essential for any business, whether starting a new adventure or expanding an being one. By following stylish practices similar as defining your business objects, conducting request exploration, creating a fiscal plan, and streamlining regularly, you can produce a winning strategy that helps you achieve

your pretensions and secure the success of
your business.

Practical Examples to Guide Your Unique Venture

7 Practical Business Adventure
exemplifications(With How- to way)
You can benefit by furnishing a service or
product that satisfies guests' requirements.
To do this, consider observing current
request trends to help you develop a unique
business idea or modify an being one.
Learning about business gambles can help
you borrow effective strategies for starting
one. In this composition, we bandy the
significance of reviewing business adventure
exemplifications, give seven business
adventure ideas, and figure way for starting
a business.

The significance of reviewing business adventure exemplifications

Reviewing business adventure exemplifications gives you sapience into the type of business to start. A business adventure is an entrepreneurial reality you can produce to induce a profit. You can also call this a small business, as it generally starts with an idea and involves limited capital or finances. This idea generally starts with a desire to satisfy a demand in the request. The business proprietor may fund this business tête-à-tête or seek investors to help with backing to grease farther development, increase brand mindfulness, and enhance gains. In exchange, the business proprietor may partake the gains with the investors.

Business adventure exemplifications

Then are business gambles you may consider starting

1. Blogging or vlogging

Blogging can be an amusing way to educate people about your areas ofinterest.However, you can blog about your experience or knowledge, If you have a particular have a high level of expertise in a certain topic.

To start blogging, post regularly to partake information online. When you gain enough followers or point callers, you may vend announcement space to brands or get auspices from companies.

Still, you can vlog rather, If you are doubtful about your jotting chops. Vlogging involves creating instructional vids to partake knowledge or information with an followership. You can upload edited content or share live vids. Being harmonious and posting content regularly are keys to sustaining this type of business.

2. Freelance graphic developer

You can start a freelance graphic design business if you are knowledgeable about using design software. This digital business requires creativity and a computer and helps other brands and individualities design ensigns, pamphlets, and other marketingmaterials.However, you may enrol in online graphic design classes, If you intend to develop your design chops. This business allows you to choose systems to work on, make a portfolio, and have a flexible work schedule.

3. Freelance Shooter

Photography may be your hobbyhorse, but it can also be a economic business adventure. Start by taking filmland that intrigue you and creating a portfolio. In accordance with what you like, photography can take many various shapes.

 You may decide to be a nature shooter who captures the world around you, similar as geographies or wildlife, or an event shooter who captures marriages, parties, and other occasions. produce a business or social media runner where you can upload your portfolio or post your work. Marketing and advertising juggernauts may also help produce mindfulness for your business and attract guests.

4. Online retail consigner

You can open an online store where you vend used particulars similar as clothes, accessories, and cabinetwork. To start this business, gather and snap the particulars you intend to vend and post them on shopping spots that connect buyers and merchandisers. It is also feasible to create a website or online store to display your products.

This business adventure allows you to make plutocrat dealing particulars you no longer use from the comfort of your home. To produce mindfulness for the business, consider running announcement juggernauts.

5. Event diary

Event planning has different specializations to choose from, including events similar as company meetings or marriages. It's also possible to pursue event planning in colorfultrades.However, consider starting a business as an event diary, If you are detail-acquainted and enjoy organizing conditioning. You can develop your chops and knowledge with online classes on effective ways to plan an event. It's frequently judicious to make your network by interacting with people and attending events when starting this career path.

6. Freelance pen

Still, consider getting a freelance pen, If you enjoy writing. You may choose a specialty or area of interest, similar as fashion, sports, or the healthcare assiduity, and produce content specific to these areas. Specializing in one area can help you find your niche request. Writing is generally economic, and you can write magazine papers, blog posts, or website dupe. produce a portfolio from published workshop or sample pieces to help showcase your chops and attract guests. It's frequently judicious to develop your jotting chops by exercising and writing regularly.

7. Packing services facilitator

Still, consider managing a quilting service rather, If you are not ready to invest capital in opening a moving company. You may mate with a moving company or work singly. There are colorful services you can consider offering. You can offer full quilting services that involve helping guests pack all of their things or partial quilting for guests who need backing with the process. An discharging service may also be salutary, as there are guests who need help discharging or settling in a new place.

How to start a business adventure
Then are way you can follow to turn your business idea into a profitable adventure:

1. Upgrade the business idea
You presumably know what you want to do if you are considering starting abusiness.However, craft a business idea by assessing your chops and interests, If you don't. A company that shares your values fosters long-term viability and expansion.

Refining your idea can help you produce a plan to guide you toward starting the business. Start the process by furnishing answers to introductory questions to help you understand how to insure the company is successful. For illustration, consider asking questions similar as " Why am I offering this service? You can learn about the business pretenses by providing an answer to this inquiry.

2. Conduct request exploration

Request exploration can help answer questions applicable to the business' success. You can discover whether openings live to turn your idea into a successful business. This process can help you gather information on your assiduity's client base and business challengers. A request check helps you learn your guests' preferences and concoct effective strategies. It's also helpful for discovering tips that may give you a competitive advantage in the request.

3. Draft a business plan

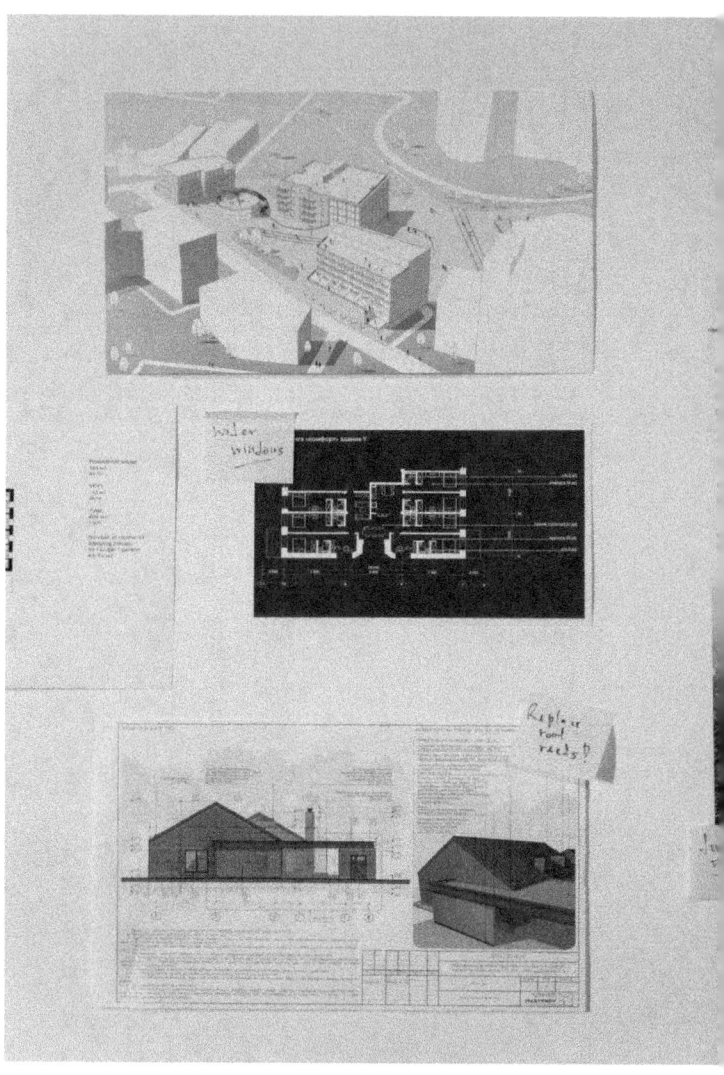

A business plan provides an overview of
your fiscal protrusions, request position, and

your unique competitive advantage. It's also helpful for demonstrating to investors or mates why they can consider investing in the business.

Produce your business plan using an online template. Then are rudiments to consider including in your business plan:

- Products and services: This section provides a detailed description of the products you intend to put into the request and the requirements they satisfy. You can also bandy what distinguishes your products or services from challengers.

- Request conditions: Produce a list of your challengers and the preferences of your target followership in this section. Determining challengers' strengths and sins can help you concoct effective marketing strategies.

- Operation: This section contains information on the business' organizational structure, crucial places, and liabilities.

- Marketing strategy: figure strategies you intend to explore to vend your products or services in this section, similar as online advertising, a website, a blog, or targeted dispatch lists.
- Fiscal plan: This section contains information on the business' financials, similar as launch- up costs. Consider stating how you intend to induce backing for the business.

4. Select the structure of your business.

Selecting a structure for your business is crucial if you plan to register it.

It influences certain aspects of the business, similar as levies and particular arrears. The most common business structure for launch-ups and small businesses is generally the limited liability company(LLC). This is a cold-blooded structure that allows businesses to enjoy the duty benefits of hookups and the legal protections of a pot. A sole procurement structure generally gives you complete power of the business and makes you responsible for its scores. You may also consider a cooperation that involves participated power with two or further people.

5. Produce an office space

Depending on the business type, produce a suitablespace.However, produce a designated plant within your home, If you can manage the business from your home. You may set this space up in your living room orbedroom.However, conduct customer- facing work, or spend time on videotape calls, If you need a further professional space.

6. Make the business

This step involves creating mindfulness for the business, maximizing profit perimeters, and satisfying guests' requirements. You may consider espousing effective marketing strategies to help you announce services to implicitcustomers.However, you may retain one or further individualities to perform tasks and reduce your workload, If applicable.

CHAPTER 4

FINANCIAL FOUNDATION

What's a fiscal foundation?

Your fiscal foundation forms the core of the life you plan to live. This foundation is the blend of habits and practices that make up your fiscal life Like the foundation of a home — a fiscal foundation requires strong structure accoutrements . Healthy saving, budgeting, and spending habits support the life you want moment and in thefuture.Without the right base, you can struggle to meet fiscal and indeed particular scores. In theU.S., poor fiscal foundations have caused numerous to struggle with living charges. Around 44 of Americans ca n't go an exigency that requires$ 400. The income of a family as a whole may suffer from poor planning. nearly 38 of homes in the U.S. have credit card debt. A poor fiscal situation can beget a person to live stipend to stipend, in malignancy of earning a decent income. also, living in habitual debt can negatively impact your internal health and produce habitual stress that damages your physical health. It might also be difficult for those who are close to you.

What are the 5 factors of a fiscal foundation?A steady income, a home of your own, or a rented space you enjoy are awful accomplishments. But a job and a home may not be enough to give and cover your fiscal security.

The following are important pieces that should form the foundation of your finances. They include:

- Budgeting
- Exigency finances
- Savings
- Investments
- A 401(k) plan

1. Budgeting

When getting on track to fiscal security, one of the first effects you should do is draft a budget. This means drawing up a list of your anticipated income and charges for the week, month, or other suitable time frames. Your foundation relies on how well you 're suitable to navigate fiscal situations. By keeping track of your spending and sticking to a budget, you can maintain control over your fiscal life. suppose of a budget as a spending companion. It keeps you within the limits of what's safe for your earning power and implicit requirements.

2. Exigency Finances

For numerous homes, one health exigency could beget a helical toward ruin. Recent checks show that only about 50 of Americans have exigency savings. Life is full of unanticipated events. The loss of a job, declining health, or major home or bus repairs can snappily put a strain on your finances. fussing about these types of events, changeable and ineluctable, puts a strain on every aspect of your health and well- being. To guard against this and gain peace of mind, fiscal counselors frequently recommend setting plutocrat away as a buffer for the unanticipated. immaculately, you save enough plutocrat to drift you over for 3- 6 months in case of an exigency, but indeed a month's charges is a meaningful thing. You can make your exigency fund through yearly benefactions. A simple yearly donation of$ 100 can be all you need to begin.

3. Savings

You can also secure your foundation by putting plutocrat away for short- term pretensions. Your checking/ savings accounts can admit any surpluses from your income. The interest rates on these accounts aid planning for a holiday, precious home device, minor auto repairs, etc.

By having a separate account, you 'll learn the benefits of keeping plutocrat away for unborn use.

4. Investments

Investments are one of the most unresistant ways to make your plutocrat grow in value over time. There are different investment options available. But to cover your interests, proper exploration should be done before deciding on a choice. This is because investments can frequently come with pitfalls. Returns on investment may also be hard to prognosticate. Common investment choices include stocks. These allow you to enjoy a portion of a pot. Another option is to purchase bonds issued by a business or the government.

Another option — collective finances, permits you to invest in a pool of security options. The investment you choose will depend on your age, fiscal situation, and particular preferences. However, there are many of options available.

As we mentioned, the requests change. So, to make the stylish choice for you, be sure to speak with a fiscal counsel or an expert in the area.

5. A 401(k) plan or other withdrawal account

Your fiscal foundation should offer support for your exigency, immediate, and unborn requirements. Taking advantage of a 401(k) plan offered as a benefit from your employer can see you through life after withdrawal. You can select standard or Convertible if your employer offers this as a choice.

During payment accommodations, you can also bandy 401k employer matching benefactions with your employer. On types, a traditional 401(k) allows you to reduce how important of your income is tested. This option makes benefactions from your pre-taxed income. The Roth 401(k) plan makes benefactions after your stipend has been tested. This option allows duty-free reductions when you retire. Your withdrawal plan stands to gain from taking advantage of either savings regard.

How to make a strong fiscal foundation

The good thing about erecting a fiscal foundation is that you don't have to be at the height of your career to get started. You could be fresh from academy, or with decades of work and life experience. At any stage you have an occasion to take action and plan for the life you would like to live. You're not required to work alone, either.

There are numerous types of fiscal coaching and comforting available. While we frequently see announcements aimed at the advanced end of wealth operation, fiscal counsels are not the only source of help. To get a home to stand establishment, concrete footing, a foundational wall, and a bottom arbor are needed for structure. also, structures must be in place to lay the root for your fiscal life.

Any good foundation takes time to make. A fiscal base is no different. The following are ways to make a strong structure:

- Get your affairs in order
- Make long- term pretensions
- Prioritize ways to cover yourself
- Pay off debts owed
- Develop a duty strategy

Get your affairs in order

Before starting a foundation, it's important to take note of the accoutrements available to make. This means your fiscal well- being requires a look at any means. Consider your buses , home, jewelry, etc exemplifications of the property you enjoy. For a full picture, you 'll also need to regard for your arrears. Pupil loans, credit card debt, and other moneybags owed will fall into this order. By writing out your means and arrears, you 're in a good position to calculate your net worth. This is worked out by adding up your means and abating your arrears. Your net worth gives a clear understanding of your fiscal status. This allows farther structure plans to take place.

Make long- term pretensions
The foundation of a home is erected with a structure in mind. In the same way, your fiscal foundation should be geared towards defined pretensions. This means making plans for your savings. For case, plutocrat set aside outside an exigency can be towards a thing. Your end could be for a down payment or other analogous purposes. pretensions can help your savings from being carried out without guidance. Your fiscal foundation can also enjoy a clear roadmap to increase your earnings. Making vittles towards fresh income aqueducts can support your fiscal life. Eventually, you should also make plans for a future where you no longer work. Beforehand on, you can identify the age you wish to retire, and how important you anticipate to have in the bank or as unresistant income.

Prioritize ways to cover yourself

Your fiscal foundation should achieve at least two effects fiscal security and stability. This means putting measures in place to cover your financial life. exigency finances offer clear benefits for unlooked-for circumstances. Job instability can be a tremendous source of stress that can indeed affect your performance. Knowing that you have other set for contingencies can ease that stress. occasionally, exigency finances can fall suddenly in furnishing the required support. Insurance content can be important in case of a health exigency, job loss, or a death in the family and supplement whatever you have in place. Your content should accommodate your earnings, life, and family requirements. A good fiscal foundation also makes it easier to watch for loved bones.

Estate planning helps keep a family's future safe. It also clarifies how additional means should be divided, or what trusts may be created. By leaving no mistrustfulness as to who's entitled to what, proper estate operation also helps save connections and avoid gratuitous stress.

Pay off debts owed

Living without debt is a top fiscal thing for numerous. This life directs your cash inflow straight to your asked requirements. An income constraint may be imposed by a home loan, balances on credit cards, or other debt.

To avoid legal issues, a lender must admit his chance of your earnings. You can, still, make your finances by organizing your debts. This should be followed by a plan to pay off advanced or lower interest debts first. With the former, you can suck the pellet to clear off the heaviest hitting loans beforehand. lower debts can also be struck out subsequently. In rear, lower interest loans can be paid off first. This allows cash inflow to accumulate for treating larger debts. Paying debts off can ameliorate the income available to meet fiscal pretensions. This approach is also inestimable for erecting your credit score.

Develop a duty Strategy

A fiscal foundation relies on smart habits. In particular, you can take advantage of openings that reduce your duty liability. borderline benefits you get from the plant like yearly auto insurance, or education charges don't get tested. The same goes for other employer benefits. Where possible, you might decide to start a business as part of your duty strategy. This allows deductions for operating costs like business outfit and marketing sweats. Consult with a duty professional before making significant changes for duty reasons. Consulting a duty expert is an investment in your future. These specialists can advise on duty- saving strategies.

Building a Solid Financial Ground for Your Small Business

How to make a Strong Financial Foundation for a New Startup? When starting a new business, it's important to have a strong fiscal foundation in place in order to insure the long- term success of the adventure.

There are a many crucial factors to erecting a strong fiscal foundation for a new incipiency:

1. Have a clear understanding of your business finances This includes knowing how important plutocrat you have coming in(profit), how important you have going out(charges), and having a clear picture of your overall fiscal picture. This will allow you to make sound fiscal opinions for your business and avoid any expensive miscalculations.

2. produce a realistic budget Once you have a clear understanding of your finances, you can produce a budget that really reflects your profit and charges. This will help you to keep your spending in check and avoid overspending on gratuitous particulars.

3. make up cash reserves It's important to have cash reserves set away in case of unanticipated charges or slow ages in your business. Having cash reserves will help to keep your business round during tough times and help you to avoid taking on gratuitous debt.

4. Invest by long- term means Long- term means, similar as property or outfit, can be salutary for a new business as they can be used as collateral for loans or can be vended if the need arises. investing in long- term means can help to give security for your business and its finances.

5. Manage debt wisely If you do need to take on debt to finance your new business,

it's important to manage it wisely. Make sure you only adopt what you need and that you have a solid plan in place for repaying the debt. Taking on too important debt can be crippling for a new business and should be avoided if possible.

By following these tips, you can make a strong fiscal foundation for your new incipiency that will help to insure its long-term success.

The significance of a Strong Financial Foundation

When starting a new business, it's essential to have a strong fiscal foundation in place. This means having the necessary backing to get the business off the ground, as well as having a solid plan in place for how the business will induce profit and gains.

One of the most important aspects of a strong fiscal foundation is having acceptable backing. This means having enough plutocrat to cover the costs of getting the business up and running, as well as any unanticipated charges that may arise. There are a many different ways to raise finances for a new business, similar as taking out loans, seeking investors, or using particular savings.

Another crucial element of a strong fiscal foundation is having a solid business plan. This plan should include a detailed analysis of the implicit request for the product or service, as well as a clear strategy for how the business will induce profit. The plan should also include fiscal protrusions for the first many times of operation, so that implicit investors can see the eventuality for profitability. erecting a strong fiscal foundation for a new business is essential to its long- term success. With acceptable backing and a solid business plan, a new business can get off to a strong launch and position itself for long- term growth.

The factors of a Strong Financial Foundation Building a strong fiscal foundation for a new incipiency requires careful planning and a solid understanding of the colorful factors that make up a sound fiscal strategy. The most important element of a strong fiscal foundation is a clear and attainable business plan. This document should lay out the company's pretensions, strategies, and mileposts in a clear and terse manner.

In addition to a well- drafted business plan, a strong fiscal foundation for a new incipiency must also include a robust marketing plan. This document should outline the company's target request, marketing strategies, and budget. Without a clear marketing plan, it'll be delicate to induce mindfulness and interest in the new company's products or services.

Another critical element of a strong fiscal foundation is a detailed and realistic budget. This document should outline all of the company's anticipated charges and income. Careful planning and a realistic assessment of the company's fiscal situation will help to insure that the incipiency has the coffers it needs to succeed. Eventually, a strong fiscal foundation for a new incipiency must include a solid understanding of the incipiency's legal scores. It's important to consult with an educated business attorney to insure that the company is in compliance with all applicable laws and regulations.

By precisely planning and considering all of these rudiments, a new incipiency can produce a strong fiscal foundation that will set the stage for long- term success.

Structure Your Business on a Solid fiscal Foundation

It's no secret that a business needs plutocrat to serve. plutocrat is the lifeblood of any enterprise, whether it's a launch- up or an established pot. The quantum of plutocrat a business has available to it frequently determines its success or failure. A business with a solid fiscal foundation is more likely to ride the storms of business and crop victorious than one that doesn't have a strong fiscal foundation.

There are several crucial factors to erecting a solid fiscal foundation for your business.

The first is to have a clear understanding of your fiscal situation. This means knowing how important plutocrat you have coming by and going out each month. It also means having a clear understanding of your means and arrears. This information will give you a clear picture of your business's fiscal health and will help you make sound opinions about where to allocate your coffers.

The alternate crucial element to erecting a solid fiscal foundation for your business is to produce a budget. A budget will help you track your charges and income so that you can see where your plutocrat is going each month. It'll also help you identify areas where you may be suitable to save plutocrat. Creating a budget is an essential step in maintaining fiscal stability for your business.

The third key element to erecting a solid fiscal foundation for your business is to establish credit lines. Credit lines give you with the finances you need to make purchases and invest in your business without having to dip into your particular savings. establishing credit lines shows creditors that you're a responsible borrower and that you have the capability to repay your debts. This can help you get better terms on unborn loans and lines of credit.

The fourth key element to erecting a solid fiscal foundation for your business is to make strong connections with your creditors. Creditors are more likely to work with you if they feel like you're secure and that you have a good history of prepayment. Building strong connections with your creditors can help you get better terms on unborn loans and lines of credit and can also help you make a good credit history.

The fifth crucial element to erecting a solid fiscal foundation for your business is to develop a contingency plan. A contingency plan is an important tool for any business proprietor because it provides a roadmap for how the business will continue to serve if commodity unanticipated happens, similar as the loss of a major client or the failure of a crucial supplier. Having a contingency plan in place will help you minimize the impact of these types of events on your business and will help you keep your business running easily. erecting a solid fiscal foundation for your business is essential to its long- term success.

By taking the time to understand your fiscal situation, establishing credit lines, erecting strong connections with creditors, and developing a contingency plan, you can insure that your business has the coffers it needs to ride any storm.

CHAPTER 5

MARKETING MAGIC

The term" marketing magic" evokes a sense of wonder and possibility. It's the art of transubstantiating ordinary effects into objects of desire, bruiting stories that enkindle imaginations, and conjuring up gests that leave a lasting print. It's not just about dealing products or services; it's about weaving spells that allure hearts and minds, guiding guests on a trip towards fulfillment. Then is how marketing can tap into this magical realm

1. Liar: The Catholicon of Enchantment
Forget boring data wastes and dry specialized slang. Marketing magic thrives on witching narratives that reverberate with feelings and bournes . Weave tales of icons prostrating challenges, of dreams coming true, of communities chancing common ground. Let your brand come a promoter in these narratives, offering results and celebrating the values your guests hold dear.

2. Sensitive temptation: A Feast for the Senses

Marketing is not just for the eyes; it's a multi-sensory experience. Transport your followership with suggestive imagery, tantalizing scents, and witching soundscapes. A beautifully drafted videotape showcasing your product in action can be more conclusive than a thousand words. Let the texture of your packaging, the meter of your music, and the aroma of your product come part of your brand's hand.

3. The Power of Community: Building a Tribe of Religionists

Marketing magic is not just about pushing products; it's about fostering connections. produce communities where your guests can partake gests , celebrate successes, and support each other. Organize events, host online forums, and offer exclusive benefits that make them feel like part of commodity special. When your guests come brand lawyers, you've truly woven your spell.

4. Personalization: The Touch of Magic In a world of mass marketing, the power of personalization is inarguable. Use data and perceptivity to knitter your dispatches, offers, and gests to individual guests. Make them feel like you understand them, like you are speaking directly to their requirements and solicitations. This substantiated touch can turn a transitory commerce into a lasting relationship.

5. The Element of Surprise: A Spark of Delight Go beyond the anticipated. Surprise your guests with unanticipated gestures, pleasurable prices, and gests that exceed their prospects. Offer free samples, host pop-up events, or produce interactive juggernauts that make them feel like they have stumbled upon commodity truly special. This element of surprise can leave a lasting print and turn guests into lifelong suckers.

Flash back, selling magic isn't about manipulation or wile; it's about creating genuine connections, eliciting feelings, and fostering a sense of wonder. It's about understanding your followership, esteeming their values, and offering them commodity truly precious in return. When you do that, you will find yourself weaving spells that not only drive deals but also make a pious community and a brand that truly resonates.

So, unleash your inner fibber, embrace the power of sensitive temptation, and make a community of religionists. With a sprinkle of creativity, a gusto of data, and a generous helping of heart, you can transfigure your marketing into commodity truly magical.

Marketing Magic

Numerous business possessors believe that simply flashing their product or service constitutes ' imprinting. ' The verity is that advertising is the veritably last step in the branding process, which begins with developing a precise position for your product or service within your competitive request. Below are some crucial studies for you as to what ' imprinting ' really is:

Branding should be seen as a endless positioning of your business to its colorful publics or target requests.

Branding must be developed with an accurate understanding of how your request actually views your product or business, not how you or your staff see yourselves. Branding is each about authorization, and what your guests or members are prepared to accept about what you say you are.

Branding – and all of your dispatches – must glorify the benefits of your product or service. Your staff must believe and live your branding if they're to deliver on the pledge of your business; staff and director education is crucial.

Branding must be done professionally to work. It's well outside the skill- set of utmost retailers and business possessors to negotiate on their own. Your time and trouble is better spent running your business, and working with a professional to ingrain and vend your business.

What are the first way in the marketing process for a business?

Define your product immolation in 3 rulings

Describe the request in which you operate

Define your client target, primary also secondary

Outline the benefits to your guests of using your product or service

Identify your 2 biggest challengers & their strengths and sins

Talk to your guests to confirm their views of why they do business with you Eventually, define your immediate,mid-term and long term pretensions

The Basics of Branding

How to ingrain your business

Produce an identity, an station, a position that stands for a set of values

Magnify your product or service with it.

Communicate it constantly through everything you do and say

Come a way of life for a pious following of guests and consumers

- Attract new guests and if you do it right, grow your business

Now, how do you get the communication out about your product or service? First, use direct deals tools:

- Public Relations
- Event Marketing
- Telemarketing
- Direct correspondence marketing
- In- store retailing and signage
- Collateral accoutrements
- Your staff and your guests

How to Get the Communication Out About Your Brand or Service Direct Deals Tools:

- Public Relations
- Event Marketing
- Telemarketing
- Direct correspondence marketing
- In- store retailing and signage
- Collateral accoutrements
- Your staff and your guests

Media Vehicles

Radio

- Pros: proximity, time spent, affordable liar

- Cons: no visual or image, low and original reach

Journals

- Pros: strong word trade/ price medium, new openings, urgency
- Cons: veritably short life, repro not strong, not an " image " medium

Magazines

- Pros: strong visual medium, utmost targeted, believable, long- continuing, reprise exposure, high reach, image and imprinting medium
- Cons: because of longer lead times, not for " trade " or " promotional " dispatches

TV

- Pros: strong impact, visual
- Cons: advanced cost medium, expensive announcement product, fractured

Out-of-door

- Pros: the perfect six- word medium, high impact, geographically picky

- Cons: demographically unselective, support medium further than a brand builder, advanced product costs

Event Marketing

- Pros: good extension for a brand, through association with right event
- Cons high cost per trade unless veritably high sticker price and periphery

Website

- Pros: great implicit
- Cons: huge competition, needs strong point, professionally and creatively erected with SEO and wide creation

Online Advertising

- Pros: targeted reach
- Cons: needs to be on a destination point with reasons for people to visit every week

Strategies and Tactics to Propel Your Brand Forward

Running an online business without a compelling brand strategy is like driving a auto without energy. Indeed a vehicle with the stylish specs fails to move forward when there's no energy.

Smart business branding is pivotal for the success and growth of any online business. Having defined brand values and a brand strategy will help you target the right followership that's authentically interested in your products and services.

A comprehensive brand strategy is an effective way to give your platoon the direction they need to make a important connection with your guests.

Before we bandy our tried- and- tested top ten branding tactics with you all, let's have a quick look at the description of the term brand strategy. We will also punctuate a many brand strategy rudiments you need to produce robust ecommerce branding tactics that help your business stand out from the crowd.

What Is Brand Strategy?

Brand strategy is a plan a brand needs to achieve specific business pretensions. A successful brand strategy revolves around practices that ameliorate client service, fiscal progress, and long- term organizational growth and performance. While this may look like an easy task at first, creating a winning brand strategy is more grueling than it appears on first prints.

Rudiments Of A Robust Brand Strategy

Still, you 're presumably looking for the stylish branding tactics to attract further business, If you 're reading this post. According to a composition published by Marketing Profs back in 2015, further than 74 of online buyers prefer brands with substantiated content on their websites. The same post revealed that " 45 of a brand's image can be attributed to what it says and how it says it ", while over 75 of consumers consider brand mindfulness a major factor that impacts their buying decision.

Now you must be wondering" what constitutes a killer imprinting strategy?"

As a general rule, a reliable brand strategy is a combination of brand purpose, brand positioning, brand image, brand personality and values, brand communication and voice, brand identity, and brand equity.

You must understand that you have to produce a branding strategy that:

reflects your brand's value

sets your brand piecemeal from others

addresses your buyer's pain points

Why Creating A Foolproof Brand Strategy Is pivotal For Your Business Success? A precisely designed brand strategy is a long-term plan that helps you achieve your pretensions and objects. Since your brand strategy impacts your online business, you have to insure it has everything that your business needs to target your client's requirements and feelings.

Without a comprehensive brand strategy, you can not spread your communication and know the values that your business reflects. In a nutshell, make sure you invest your time and other coffers in creating a killer brand strategy that can help you attract and engage further guests for your brand.

How To produce A Winning Brand Strategy?

Creating a brand strategy is a multi-step process. Flash back, it takes time and coffers to produce a strategy that converts over the span of time. Then's a step- by- step companion to creating a successful branding strategy.

Define Your Purpose

The first step to creating a successful brand strategy is to know the purpose of your business creation AKA brand identity. relating your brand identify is a critical factor. Besides egregious benefits, similar as ROI, you must concentrate on what value you want to give to your target followership. After determining the purpose of your business's actuality, it's time to pay attention to the environment in which your business operates.

Understand The Environment

No online business operates in a vacuum. Anyhow of how unique your products and offers are, your business has challengers. You have a direct relationship with your challengers if they 're performing better than you, your deals will go down, and vice versa. So keeping an eye on how your challengers are performing in the business world is more essential than ever. For this, you have to conduct a contender analysis to see what others are doing to succeed in a business.

Setting SMART objects

The coming step is to produce SMART(Specific, Measurable, Attainable, Applicable, and Timely) objects grounded on the information you gathered in the first and alternate way.

Again, we 're not talking about fiscal objects only. Your business objects must also touch on brand values and comprehensions, product exploration and development, and day- to- day business tasks.

Produce A Plan

After setting SMART objects, it's time to virtually work on a strategy that's in line with your overall business pretensions and objects.

In this step, you have to produce a brand strategy that highlights your:

- charge/ Vision
- Brand tone
- Policy expression encircling your brand values
- Investment plans for unborn business expansion

Test, Tweak And Develop

The last step is to test your brand strategy and see if it matches your objects and prospects. Flash back, a brand strategy is n't commodity stationary. You have to work on it to make it more perfect and affect- driven.

Test your approaches using different available tools online, identify your sins, and make adaptations to drive the asked results.

At this point, you must have a clear understanding of what brand strategy is and what rudiments you need to work on to get it right. To make this entire discussion more comprehensive and accessible, we've created a list of the stylish branding tips to grow your business.

Top 10 Branding Tactics To Help Your Business Stand Out From The Crowd

1. Identify Your Target followership

Businesses that conduct methodical exploration on their target followership grow briskly and achieve further ROI than businesses that don't get this step right.

Trying to know your target followership will help you more understand your client's buying preferences, perspectives, and needs. With this information at hand, you can produce a communication that resonates with your prospects.

In addition to that, you can also identify your establishment's strengths and sins, allowing you to take lower threat on your ecommerce marketing strategy.

Besides different tools, you can also produce buyer personas to guide your opinions. Do in- depth exploration and determine every detail about people who 're likely to buy your products- their position, age, buying preferences, age, gender, and more.

2. Set norms

All big brands, including Apple, Coca- Cola, and Samsung, have unique branding individualities and norms. Indeed if the brand launches commodity different from its usual product range, people have no difficulty relating the brand.

You must also set norms for your brand that differentiates them from the rest of the competition. There are 4 crucial areas you should concentrate on while setting brand norms.

Totem

A totem is a visual trademark that reflects the unique nature of your business. In certain cases, a totem also acts as a status symbol. Let's take the illustration of Mercedes Benz, Rolex, or Nike. People identify these brands with their unique ensigns and taglines.

Make sure you hire the services of a professional totem developer to produce a unique totem for your brand. The placement and size of your totem should remain harmonious on all marketing accoutrements , including TV advertisements, social media advertisements, magazine advertisements, banners, flyers , and other marketing accoutrements .

Plates

It's also critical to use the same graphic rudiments across different channels to help your consumers flash back your brand.

Color Palette
Analogous to graphic rudiments, the color palette you 're using across different platforms helps elicit feelings.

Sources
Pick one or two sources and insure you 're using them constantly throughout your marketing accouterments .

3. Maintain A harmonious Brand Voice
Analogous to visual rudiments on your website and other marketing material, your brand voice should remain the same across different platforms. Selecting the voice of your brand is the goal.
For case, if you 're running a business that serves kiddies or fashion suckers, you can choose a tone that's quirky, light- hearted, and fun.

On the wise side, if your target followership is mentally ill individualities or cases, your tone should reflect your products and services. After deciding your brand tone, the coming step is creating a brand story and acclimatized dispatches that are compelling enough to catch your target followership's attention and attract deals.

4. Award Your pious guests

According to a Harvard Business School check, a 5 increase in client retention results in over to 95 ROI. As an online business, it's your responsibility to concoct strategies that not only help you meet your client's prospects but exceed them. When you under- pledge and over-deliver, your guests will come your brand lawyers.

Then are a many effects you can do to earn a pious client

Address client enterprises before they come a conflict give excellent client service through live converse agents and chatbots

Offer client fidelity programs Gather client feedback and information using checks

5. make Your Marketing Toolkit

After erecting a website, you need to work on an each- inclusive marketing toolkit. Your marketing toolkit should include deals wastes, a to- the- point pitch sundeck, and your company's folder.

Successful businesses also include vids pressing your business's overview, details about your business mates, and case studies.

You can use these marketing toolkits for brand development and promoting your business.

6. Research Current Trends

Still, the first step is to conduct request exploration to identify the rearmost assiduity trends, If you 're planning to start a business from scrape.

Indeed if you have an established business, you should include request exploration as part of your business development function as it'll help you keep your business in line with the evolving trends.

You can buy exploration reports available on the web. Also, if buying precious reports is n't an option, there's plenitude of information available on the internet that you can use before getting started.

7. Use Influencers

A Neilsen report reveals that over 77 of druggies prefer to invest in a brand that's recommended by someone they trust.

Using an influencer marketing strategy is an effective way to reach out to your target followership. For this, you have to define your influencers grounded on applicability and reach.

Engage with these influencers through their social media content and make connections with them using CRM tools.

8. Trademark Your Brand

With further and further businesses entering the digital world to do business, coming up with an seductive business name is getting further grueling day by day. Your brand identity is primarily represented by your name.

Still, make sure you cover it through a trademark, If you have formerly resolved this riddle and decided on a perfect name for your online business.

9. Develop A Strong Content Marketing Strategy

The biggest challenge for ecommerce stores is to keep coming up with fresh content ideas that hook their anthology's interest.

Luckily there are colorful happy idea creator tools that can help you overcome this challenge and induce compelling content ideas for your eCommerce stores. Produce a stoner-friendly website that explains what your brand offers to the client. Include action- driven CTAs at the right places to encourage your callers to take timely action.

You must also have a devoted blog section on your website where you can contribute precious style- to papers, blog posts, reviews, trending assiduity news, and more.

10. Apply, Track, And Acclimate

Last but not least, whatever strategies you have created and enforced, do n't leave them on their own. Make sure you track and test them from time to time using the stylish available online coffers. Also, make the needed adaptations to keep your branding strategy in line with your business's long-term and short- term pretensions.

CHAPTER 6

CUSTOMER CONNECTIONS

Client connection can be defined as the relationship you make with your client outside of your product or service. It may be the most important part of the client trip.

In a 2018 study, Sow Social set up that " nearly two thirds(64) of consumers want brands to connect with them.

Your guests expect you and your team to remain available to them in addition to the outcome your product offers. They want your support platoon to be there for them when commodity goes wrong. They want your deals platoon to consult and educate them on how to stylish use your products and services.

They 're looking for a particular connection — a mortal connection. They want to feel like further than just a case or ticket or a number added to your profit.

Why is client connection important?
Furnishing a mortal connection to your guests creates fidelity by furnishing a great client experience. And that's not only good for your guests. It's good for business.

The same study from Sprout Social set up that " Investing in connections with consumers directly impacts business profit and strengthens client fidelity. When guests feel connected to brands, further than half of consumers(57) will increase their spending with that brand and 76 will buy from them over a contender. Establishing a connection is crucial for both your visitors and your company, so give it top priority.

6 stylish practices to make client connections effectively Connection does n't be by accident in business. It needs to be

purposeful. Then are six ways to effectively connect with guests.

1. Make every client feel unique

Reluctantly set up that 79 of guests say " substantiated service is more important than substantiated marketing. "

But how do you do that? First and foremost, deliver great client service to everyone that connections your support platoon. To show great client service, respond instantly to your guests. Show empathy toward their issue. Do your stylish to understand where they 're comingfrom.However, reach out to them directly and offer to resolve the situation, If someone gives you negative feedback. You can indeed add empathy to your quality assurance(QA) scorecard to keep your platoon responsible.

Simple sweats make a big difference, similar as:

Using the client's name during communication

Bodying dispatch templates to not sound so " commercial "

Making sure issues are resolved instantly

Taking way like these help your guests feel valued and prioritized when they need your backing. occasionally that's all it takes to produce a meaningful connection.

2. Learn about each customer

UVL Uppuluri, Head of client Success at Cribl, says we should " watch about the guests as individualities as these ca n't be faked by shallow kindness or be driven only to achieve specific business or relinquishment issues. "

It's crucial for your offers staff to keep an eye on those present as individuals rather than just as potential customers. Use customer meetings to ask good questions and show a genuine interest in your guests ' lives and interests. Get to know them beyond just their business requirements.

Having a good deals operations process can help with this. Deals ops can make it easier to save and recall client details in your CRM and can grease good handoffs from marketing to deals to client success.

3. Attend to every client issue

This may sound egregious, but your guests want an amazing experience when they communicate your support platoon. They want their problems answered easily and snappily.

" Wow " your guests by getting to the root of their issues and also working them presto. When you 're choosing pretensions, set speed of answer, handle rate, and handle time criteria above the assiduity standard and also hold your platoon responsible to them.

still, consider getting help from an expert outsourced support platoon to enable you to ameliorate your client service as you gauge, If that sounds like a challenge. Fostering a sense of cooperation and fellowship between your deals platoon and support platoon can also help produce a harmonious positive experience and connection for your guests.

4. Touch base with your guests constantly

Infrequently touching base can harm your relationship with your guests. They may forget about you, or worse yet, suppose they do n't really count to you.

Rather, communicate your guests constantly to touch base. Try effects like:

Having your deals platoon reach out shortly after a trade to check in and answer questions

Set up scalable processes for your client success platoon to regularly reach out and offer visionary help

Have your marketing platoon shoot regular emails with stylish practices and stories from your assiduity.

When you release a new product, reach out proactively to see if your guests want to test or buy it.

Conditioning like this keep your company top of mind, and if you can execute on them in a individualized way, can also help produce stronger connections with your guests.

5. Ask for feedback

Feedback is pivotal to creating client connections. Asking for feedback shows your guests you value their opinion and want to ameliorate the service you give them. Then's the catch If you ask for feedback, you also need to find ways to act upon it.

Asking for feedback can be structured or unshaped. It can be in informal exchanges or through automated tools. Then are some exemplifications

Shoot client checks after relations with your client support platoon Have your deals platoon ask questions about how your guests like your product and how they 're seeing value from it shoot out palpitation checks to your guests(and incentivize them with if necessary) Stress with your guests that you always want their honest feedback. Indeed if it's feedback that's tough for you to hear, when you admit it with grace and openness, your guests will take notice.

6. Exceed guests prospects

One of the stylish ways to produce a connection with your guests is to exceed their prospects. At Peak Support, we say you should make exceeding prospects your charge.

They say you only get one chance to make a first print on someone, but that's not always the case. Each commerce you have with your guests is a separate occasion to leave a positive lasting print on them. The sum of all those relations forms your client's overall experience with your brand.

Hub spot gives a particular connection illustration of a regular client at a Mongolian Grill eatery. They forgot their portmanteau so could n't pay after eating. The eatery honored them as a regular client and told them it was on the house that day. That's an amazing way to exceed a client's prospects and produce brand fidelity.

Ask yourself how you can exceed your guests ' prospects in a analogous way. Could you empower your support platoon to sometimes surprise guests with a free month of your product?

Enhancing your client connections
Connecting with guests is easier said than done, but it starts with putting and keeping — your guests first. A client- centric mindset means everything you do is organized around your guests. The lucre to being purposeful with client connection is the creation of lifelong connections and high brand fidelity.

At Peak Support, we can give the help and moxie you need to make long- lasting client connections. communicate us moment for further word on how we can help support your being brigades!

Establishing Meaningful Relationships for Long-Term Success

We all want to be better. A better man, a better hubby or swain, a better father, a better entrepreneur. The verity is that, when it comes to being better and being successful, the connections we make play a pivotal part. In this post, I partake nine way you can follow to make better, meaningful, long- lasting particular and professional connections.

1. Be Honest

Anyhow of the type of relationship you want to make, you owe it to yourself and to others to be honest. When you 're true to yourself and know what you want, cultivating inconceivable connections, which are going to profit you and others, is going to be easier.

2. Put Others Before Yourself

When I canvassed Mark Sieverkropp, who Forbes named one of 50 Professional Networking Experts to Watch in 2015, he talked about the " secret sauce for building any kind of durable relationship.

No fancy words or mind tricks then just one word listening. You may have an docket, but you have to make sure that you 're a listener first.

3. How to Always Make a Great First Impression

Let's be honest I 'm enough sure you had been on your way to an event, a party or a conference, and had been allowing of how you could make a great first print.

When it comes to this aspect, numerous people concentrate on what they 're going to say first. still, as my friend Jordan Harbinger-co-host of The Art of Charm-explained in a podcast interview we did, first prints have nothing to do with what you say.

First prints are non-verbal, they be when someone notices you and makes a first assessment of you.

Then there is what you can do: keep your head over, shoulders back, casket up and have a nice smile on your face.However, confident and friendly, people are going to treat you that way, If you look open.

4. Make Everybody You Meet Feel Drink

You may be wondering, " How am I going to do that? "

Well, my friend, the answer is easier than you suppose. And ties into what I've bandied in point# 2. still, you need to pay attention to them and show interest, If you want to make every single person you meet feel welcome.

Do n't be hysterical to ask them about themselves- people love when others show interest in them. Are they saying commodity intriguing? Great! Make sure to repeat some of that, as you 're opining what they've just told you. In utmost cases, showing interest is going to affect in the other person's genuine interest in you and your particular story.

5. Focus on the Positive

In his new book Are You Completely Charged? The 3 Keys to Amping Your Work and Life best- dealing author, heartiness and health expert Tom Rath talks about a simple thing you can do to ameliorate the quality of your connections.

We all have relations throughout our day with our partner or mate, with our children, with our associates and business mates, with the machine motorist, etc. But what can you do to ameliorate their nature?

The answer is simple focus on having more positive relations.

On the 360 Entrepreneur Podcast, Rath explained the significance of this aspect " A single negative commerce has an impact that's more important than that of five positive relations.

What then can you do to address that?

For starters, pay attention and put emphasis on people's strengths and triumphs. When talking to someone try and concentrate on their positive traits.

You shouldn't ignore the negative sides of your relations, but immaculately you would want to follow an 80- 20 rule. Where 80 of your relations look at positive aspects, and only the 20 deals with negative bones.

6.(Be a coadjutor and) Take It One Step farther

How can you stand out from the crowd and make sure others flash back you? Whether you 're floundering to make meaningful particular or professional connections, there's a good chance that you following the mass. Being like everybody differently and doing what everybody additional's exploit, has an impact on that.

Perhaps you want to impress the woman you 're courting(flash back , be honest to yourself) or maybe you would like to connect with leaders in your assistance on social media or at the coming conference you 're both going to attend.

Keep in mind that we all need help with commodities. Your date may be new in city and in need of help getting to know the place.However, your woman

 might be pursuing a specific dream, and you could help turning that into reality, If you 're wedded.

Influencers in your niche always appreciate exposure. Your help could come in the form of an Amazon review of their new book, a blog post mentioning them or an assignation to be a guest on your podcast, for illustration.

Stay honest with yourself and try to figure out ways you can stand out by taking it one step further and help others- each without having a particular docket in mind.

7. Don't Be hysterical to Show Your excrescences

Occasionally, you need to put your pride away, open up and admit you have made a mistake.

Why?

We all want to be perfect, the nascence man, but the reality is that vulnerability allows us to connect with those we 're talking to on an emotional position.

In other words, by being honest, admitting you made a mistake and by apologizing, you show a big strength your capability to admit your excrescencies. Flash back, showing your vulnerable side is a sign of openness and honesty to the other person.

8. Follow- Up

Particularly when it comes to business connections, people take the vault and break the ice. They introduce themselves, sputter for a little why, exchange business cards and contact information

And leave it at that,

Networking, relationship- structure expert, and former White House Writer John Corcoran frequently stresses the significance of following up. For your business connections, you can do that using a CRM(client relationship operation) software like Contactually, for case.

This is going to make sure that you get the most out of the relationship with your guests, your peers and leaders in your assiduity.

For your particular connections, you can use a fashion I learned from Mark Sieverkropp. You can break down the connections in your phone or dispatch address book in alphabetical order and devote a many twinkles of each week to reach out to them. This week, for illustration, you could concentrate on people whose last name starts with the letters A, B andC. Next week, D, E, and F,etc.

This will make sure that you 're not going to be forgotten by people, and will keep your connections an ongoing thing.

9. Leave Everything and Everybody More Than You set up Them There's plenitude of tips and tricks I could partake withyou.However, meaningful, long-continuing connections, If you want to make better.

CHAPTER 7

OPERATIONS UNVEILED

Welcome to the heartbeat of your small-scale business, where operations take center stage, and every detail plays a vital role in the grand performance. In this chapter, we're not just unveiling operations; we're revealing the rhythm, the soul, and the human touch that make your business a symphony. where everything works together to create a seamless performance.

Think of your day-to-day operations as the instruments in an orchestra—each one contributing to the overall harmony. From managing inventory to fine-tuning workflows, we'll explore how these elements come together to create a business melody that resonates with both you and your customers.

Now, let's talk about the intricate dance of your supply chain. Imagine it as a ballet, where every step is crucial for a flawless performance. We'll navigate the choreography of supply chain management, ensuring that your products pirouette smoothly from creation to delivery.

But what's a symphony without a cast of characters? Your team is the ensemble, and effective communication is the conductor. We'll explore ways to enhance teamwork, turning your operation into a well-coordinated play where everyone knows their part. It's about fostering a culture where each member feels valued, contributing to the success of the entire composition.

In the ever-evolving world of business, innovation is your avant-garde soloist. We'll discuss how embracing technology and modern methodologies adds dynamic elements to your symphony. It's not just about staying current; it's about leading the orchestra into uncharted territories, creating a business performance that captivates and inspires.

By the end of this chapter, you won't just see operations as a necessity; you'll recognize them as the driving force behind your business symphony. So, grab your conductor's baton, and let's unveil the magic in the rhythm of your operations. Get ready to create a symphony that leaves a lasting impression on your audience and sets your business apart in the grand concert of success!

Practical Tips for Efficient and Effective Business Operations

SIX WAYS TO INCREASE YOUR BUSINESS 'S EFFICIENCY

A business that runs efficiently is much more likely to find uninterrupted success over the long- term. effectiveness boosts productivity and can give you an edge in moment's competitive request. Then are six ideas that can help your business come more effective.

1. Automate Operations

One of the stylish ways to boost effectiveness is to automate as numerous tasks as possible. As tech has bettered over the times, it has come easier to have programs handle numerous business tasks that would have taken a great deal further time in history.

" Assess the operations of your business, and invest in software that automates as numerous of those processes as possible so you can get the mundane work done efficiently and your workers can concentrate on other tasks," says Victor Snyder atBusiness.com.1" further of these results are available now than ever ahead because of the current demand for mobile structure, and that means this is an excellent time to reassess which job functions can be excluded so you can more allocate time to more burning requirements that bear the critical study of a mortal worker."

As you estimate your current business processes, explore what's on the software request for specific areas of your operation.However, consider contracting with a inventor to produce your own program, If you ca n't find what you need.

2. Delegate and Consolidate

Tasks Increased effectiveness starts with you, the business proprietor, and that means knowing when to delegate tasks so your focus can be where it needs to be.

Walter Murphy states at the SCORE program, "You'll have to delegate if you want to manage your firm more efficiently.

Take the time to learn your workers' strengths and sins so that you can delegate more effectively. Put checks and balances in place so that you can cover the processes in the morning and relax control over time. Eventually, trust your platoon to negotiate their places. Delegation puts responsibility on your platoon and can help them come more invested in the success of your business." 2

Some tasks may also be suitable to be consolidated. Look for redundancies and gratuitous way in your processes.However, you might be suitable to give both to the same person, who'll be suitable to complete them more efficiently, If someone is formerly performing one task that's related to another being performed by someone differently.

3. Ameliorate Time Management

Delegating tasks is one part of time operation, but it's not the whole story. There are effects you can do on a diurnal base to insure you're making the most effective use of your own time. Stick to a schedule when possible, maintain a prioritized to- do list and produce time blocks for different aspects of your work. Be sure to include flexible time to handle unanticipated circumstances or to give yourself time to finish tasks that took longer than anticipated.

4. Look for Outsourcing openings

Important like robotization, outsourcing some places can also help your company run more efficiently, freeing up your core platoon's time to handle tasks most applicable for their skill sets. You can outsource just about any business function, from secretary to marketing and from deals to client service. There are plenitude of spots online where you can find freelancers eagerly awaiting their coming gig.

5. Hear to Your platoon

Members of your platoon are dealing with the everyday processes and complications of the job. Their perspectives are incredibly precious when it comes to ideas on how to increase productivity and effectiveness as they pertain to their specific places. It's possible that as the business proprietor you only have a broad idea of what goes into a given task. workers generally want to perform well and make their own lives lightly at the same time. Increased effectiveness will allow them to do both. Consider starting an impulses program that rewards workers who present good ideas to increase effectiveness in their job processes. also, it's your job to hear to what they've to say, and if you agree with their assessment, you might be suitable to put the right bus in stir to make these advancements be.

6. Noway Stop Improving
Effectiveness can be bettered over and over again as time goes on. Do not get too set in your ways because processes can change and evolve. estimate your effectiveness on a regular schedule to make sure you 're keeping up with trends and technology.

CHAPTER 8

OVERCOMING CHALLENGES

Ahoy there! Welcome to the sometimes stormy, always unpredictable seas of entrepreneurship. In this chapter, we're going to tackle the challenges head-on, like seasoned sailors navigating through rough waters. Think of it as your trusty guide for when the waves get high and the winds blow strong.

First off, let's be real: challenges are part of the adventure. They're not roadblocks but rather twists and turns in your entrepreneurial journey. We'll chat about the common hurdles that entrepreneurs face, from budget storms to unexpected market waves. Consider this chapter as your onboard friend, helping you steer through the challenges with confidence.

Ever felt like your business ship is sailing against the wind? We've all been there. We'll talk about strategies to not only adapt but thrive in the face of change. It's about adjusting your course when things get choppy, finding new paths, and turning challenges into opportunities. Think of it as your survival kit for the ups and downs of entrepreneurship.

But let's not just talk theory. We'll dive into real stories from fellow entrepreneurs who faced storms and emerged stronger. Their experiences are like beacons, lighting the way and showing you that challenges are just a part of the journey. They're opportunities to learn, grow, and make your business ship even sturdier.

We'll also dig into the importance of having a resilient mindset – your anchor in rough seas. It's about staying steady when the waves are high. We'll explore practical tips for maintaining mental strength and emotional resilience as you navigate the unpredictable waters of entrepreneurship.

By the end of this chapter, you won't just see challenges as obstacles; you'll see them as moments of growth. You'll be ready to face the storms, adjust your sails, and keep sailing towards the horizon of success. So, let's hoist those sails, ride the waves, and conquer the challenges of entrepreneurship together!

Turning Hurdles into Stepping Stones on Your Entrepreneurial Path

Alright, friend, let's dive deeper into this journey of ours. In this chapter, we're going to explore the twists and turns of entrepreneurship and how every obstacle, every hiccup, can be transformed into a stepping stone on your path to success.

Imagine you're on a hike, and suddenly there's this massive boulder blocking your way. It might seem like a roadblock, but what if I told you it's not there to stop you? It's a challenge, and by overcoming it, you're not just moving forward—you're gaining a foothold for something greater. That's what we're going to unravel in this chapter.

We'll talk about the hurdles every entrepreneur faces. You know, those moments where things seem tough – financially, in the market, you name it. But here's the twist: these challenges are opportunities for growth. We'll chat about how, with the right mindset, you can turn them into stepping stones toward your goals.

Think of your business journey as a dynamic trail with hills and valleys. Some challenges might be steep hills, but we're going to learn how to climb them. We're not just bypassing obstacles; we're figuring out how to make each one a part of your unique story.

And challenges? They're not roadblocks; they're secret passageways. We'll dive into strategies for not only conquering them but making them work for you. It's like turning stumbling blocks into solid foundations for your business. This chapter is your roadmap to seeing every hurdle as a chance to evolve, learn, and make your business even more resilient.

We'll share stories – real stories from real entrepreneurs who faced challenges head-on and came out on top. Their experiences are like guideposts, showing you that every hurdle is a stepping stone to your own success story.

So, grab a cup of your favorite drink, get cozy, and let's turn these hurdles into stepping stones on our epic journey through entrepreneurship. Because, my friend, the path might be challenging, but the view from the top is absolutely worth it.

CHAPTER 9

SCALING YOUR SUCCESS

Imagine your success as a tiny seed, bursting with potential but needing the right conditions to flourish. Scaling your success is nurturing that seed, providing the sunlight, water, and nutrients it needs to grow into a towering oak, sturdy and resilient against the winds of change.

But how do you scale success? How do you take that initial spark and transform it into something impactful and enduring? Here are some key steps to guide your ascent:

1. Lay a Strong Foundation:

Identify your core values: What principles guide your decisions and actions? Knowing your values ensures your growth remains aligned with your essence.

Define your vision: Where do you see yourself in the future? A clear vision provides direction and motivates you to keep moving forward.

Build a solid team: Surround yourself with talented and passionate individuals who complement your skills and share your vision.

2. Embrace Continuous Learning:

Never stop acquiring knowledge: Read, attend workshops, network with experts – stay hungry for new ideas and perspectives.

Sharpen your skills: Invest in personal and professional development to become the best version of yourself.

Adapt and be flexible: The world is constantly changing, so be prepared to adjust your strategies and embrace new opportunities.

3. Delegate and Empower:

As you grow, you can't do everything yourself. Learn to delegate tasks effectively and empower your team to take ownership and make decisions. This frees you to focus on strategic initiatives and long-term vision.

4. Measure and Analyze:

Data is your friend. Track your progress, analyze your results, and identify areas for improvement. Don't be afraid to experiment and iterate, refining your approach based on what works and what doesn't.

5. Build Strong Relationships:

Success is rarely achieved in a vacuum. Foster meaningful connections with clients, partners, and mentors. These relationships can provide invaluable support, resources, and opportunities for growth.

6. Celebrate Milestones and Embrace Challenges:

Scaling success is a journey, not a destination. Take time to celebrate your achievements, big and small. And remember, challenges are inevitable. View them as opportunities to learn and grow, to become even stronger and more resilient.

Remember, scaling your success is not a linear process. There will be times of rapid growth followed by periods of plateauing or even setbacks. But by staying focused on your core values, nurturing your knowledge, building strong relationships, and embracing the inevitable challenges, you can transform that tiny seed into a towering oak, a testament to your dedication and resilience.

So, set your sights on the horizon, plant the seeds of your ambition, and embark on the thrilling journey of scaling your success. The world awaits the shade of your mighty oak.

Taking Your Small Business to New Height

Whether you 've been in business for a long time, or you're a new incipiency, sole owner, or an independent contractor, there are a number of way that any small business proprietor can take as they grow their business and ameliorate their nethermost line.

1. Continuously estimate your business plan The frugality and request trends are in a constant state of flux, so it's important to periodically review your business plan to make sure it's up to date with what your business provides and what the request demands. For illustration, during the

coronavirus epidemic, businesses dealt with force chain dislocations, fleetly changing demands, and government- ordered shutdowns. For illustration, food and libation businesses went through tremendous bouleversement during the epidemic. numerous of them experimented with take-out windows, food deliveries, and out-of-door dining. Some reduced their menu options and cut their hours because of force and staffing issues.

Numerous retailers faced analogous challenges, especially from the increase in online shopping and government restrictions during the epidemic.

Effects to consider for your business plan include:

The demand for what your company offers and how it's changed.

How your assiduity is doing compared to the rest of the frugality.

What changes have your challengers made, what they offer and their marketing approach?

Have you met your deals and profit protrusions?

What's your client experience and retention like, and do you need to change your approach?

What chances do you have for success?

What's your marketing strategy?

2. Enhance your branding

Branding is what sets you piecemeal from the competition. It's how you define your own business, what your company represents to your guests, and it helps determine how you vend your business. It's an important part of any small business growth strategy and marketing plan. To ameliorate your branding, it's a good idea to start with your guests. Figure out what specifically appeals to them about your company and the services you provide.

They can help you define what sets you piecemeal from the competition. Your brand may include the tone and voice you use in your dispatches with implicit guests, your totem and tagline. Is your tone formal or informal? Did your catchphrase clearly convey the core values of your company? These are effects to consider when establishing or enriching your brand. Once you have your brand linked, use it as a companion for all of your dispatches and marketing sweats. This includes advertising, social media posts, emails, and your company's website.

3. Focus on your client connections

A pious client base is pivotal in keeping your business profitable and reaching new guests. Of course, client retention starts with prioritizing client service and taking care of those who affect your business. A client relations operation(CRM) program can help you maintain your client base as you work to acquire new guests.

One of the benefits of a CRM program is it allows you to collect contact information from your guests. A client who's willing to subscribe up to your dispatch list and admit announcements about your business, client abatements, and new immolations is more likely to affect your establishment and to tell their musketeers.

You can also learn what your frequent guests like utmost about your business and highlight this in your elevations.

Post meaningful information

Your content should be useful to implicit guests. For illustration, a cleaning business might offer advice on drawing or dealing with stains. An IT company might give information on guarding computer systems from being addressed, or the rearmost malware trends.

Engage with guests

Your content marketing sweats should invite participation and responses, similar as posing a question or encouraging guests to respond to social media posts that involve your products or services, this offers a chance to engage with guests and spread mindfulness about your business. You might encourage guests to post intriguing filmland of themselves visiting your business or enjoying your products and services. For illustration, pet care businesses could invite people to post filmland of their faves while mentioning the business. It's pivotal for your business to cover your social media exertion and any mentions of your business, whether a client offers positive feedback or complaints. Engaging with and addressing any enterprises lets people know that you value your guests and your business's character.

Offer client impulses To encourage client engagement, your business might offer a free comp or a reduction to a client who posts about your business on socialmedia.However, they could really help you take your business to the coming position and reach your target followership, If any of your current guests are social media influencers. You might offer a comp or reduction to the client whose post receives the most commerce on social media, have the winner chosen aimlessly

each month, or by your staff. Of course, those who affect your business and are active on social media can also help you by posting favorable reviews online. To indeed go a step further, you could produce a client fidelity program for those who affect your business. Those in the food and libation diligence could offer free or blinked particulars grounded on how numerous times a client visits their business. For illustration, a bakery might offer a free cupcake to frequent guests on their birthday, or a eatery might offer a birthday reduction or a free cate
with regale.

Post constantly

No matter where you post content, whether it's on your own website, an dispatch newsletter, or social media, it's a good idea to give this content on a harmonious base. This increases the chance that people will engage with what you 're posting and ameliorate brand mindfulness for your company.

For illustration, landscaping business could offer advice on lawncare, fertilizing, and guarding shops from pests, severe rainfall, and complaint.

4. Scale your operations wisely

Presumably the stylish time to expand your business is when the frugality is growing, either nationally or in your particular area. Keep an eye on trends within your assiduity and watch for openings. You should also keep an eye out for new businesses that might contend with your own. Real estate has ages of high growth, followed by retardations. The same is true for the construction and constricting fields. Trying to expand your business during a depression in the frugality would be like swimming against the drift. As you grow your business, it's also important that you maintain your client base and keep delivering the same quality of products and services that they anticipate. still, you 'll need to stay on top of social media trends, any new platforms that come popular, If your client base is active online.

5. Streamline your processes Take a close look at your business to find ways to ameliorate your effectiveness. Exist any devices, software, or procedures that would enable your company to grow without sacrificing quality?
numerous tasks in the manufacturing sector can be bettered with investments in outfit, robotization, and hand training. In the online retail sector, you might consider which products are most profitable, and utmost asked , by your guests. It's also important to cover any products or services that are loss leaders and draw guests to your website.

6. Ameliorate your online presence Any website or social media presence must keep up with the times. Social media platforms can rise and fall inimportance.However, you 'll need to stay on top of social media trends, any new platforms that come popular, If your client base is active online. You might

STARTING SMALL-SCALE BUSINESS

compare your website and social media use to how other businesses in your field use them, especially your closest challengers. You 'll need to cover how well you 're performing online. This includes how people pierce your point, how important time they spend there, and whether they buy commodity or leave. Google Analytics can help you keep track of this data and any changes in criteria .

7. insure that you have the right insurance content As your business expands, it's important to dissect your pitfalls on a regular base and make sure you 're completely covered with the right types of small business insurance. General liability insurance General liability insurance covers common business pitfalls similar as a client injury on your property, damage to a client's property, and advertising injury. marketable property insurance marketable property insurance covers the physical position of your business, supplies, and outfit in case it's stolen, lost, or damaged. However, you

may need to increase your marketable property content, If your business is growing and you 're expanding your structure or moving to a larger bone.

Business proprietor's policy(BOP)

For those who need both general liability content and marketable property insurance, a business proprietor's policy packets both contents together and is generally less precious than buying each policy independently.

Professional liability insurance

Professional liability insurance, also known as crimes and deletions insurance(E&O), covers the cost of customer suits and agreements over wrong work, similar as missing a deadline for making a expensive mistake. This content is known as professional liability when used by accountants, adjudicators, advisers , and masterminds. crimes and deletions content is used by real estate agents, duty preparers, IT professionals, and insurance agents. In the medical field, this content is known as medical malpractice insurance.

Marketable bus insurance

Marketable bus insurance is needed in utmost countries for businesses that enjoy vehicles. It covers legal bills, medical charges, and property damage if a business vehicle is involved in an accident.

Workers presentation insurance

Workers presentation insurance is needed in utmost countries for businesses with one or further workers. It's also needed for sole possessors in unsafe professions, similar as roofing.

Cyber insurance

Cyber insurance, also known as cyber liability insurance, covers the precious costs of dealing with a data breach or vicious software attack at your business. This content includes the cost of client announcements, credit monitoring, legal freights, and forfeitures. Cyber insurance also includes third- party cyber pitfalls, similar as a client suing you for failing to cover their data.

Business interruption insurance

Business interruption insurance covers your lost profit, business charges, and relocation costs in case your business is forced to close temporarily because of a disastrous event, similar as a fire or flood tide.

8. Make smart backing investments

Expanding your business will presumably bear investors or loans to give the investment capital you 'll need. You 'll need a business plan and fiscal data that indicate your current fiscal situation, former growth numbers, and vaticinations. Make sure your cash inflow and gains are steady before launching an expansion. Creating a cautious budget is also a smart idea.

You 'll need to have enough finances to cover any contingencies, similar as your growth estimates not performing as anticipated.

The Small Business Administration offers SBA- backed loans for small business possessors. These include:

7(a) loans

7(a) loans are small business loans of over to$ 5 million that can be used for:

Acquiring, refinancing, or perfecting real estate

Working capitol

Debt refinancing Buying new ministry, outfit, cabinetwork, and supplies

Changing power

504 loans

504 loans offer long- term fixed rate backing of over to$5.5 million for investing in fixed means, similar as Buying land and structures New construction Improving structures and structure, similar as thoroughfares and parking lots Buying long- term ministry and outfit Microloans Microloans of over to$ 50,000 can be used to rebuild, form, or ameliorate your small business. They can be

used to give working statehouse, buying inventories, ministry, and outfit. They can not be used to pay off being debt or buy real estate. Other backing options Your other options for financing a small business expansion include low- interest credit cards, bank loans, and crowdfunding platforms. You might also consider chancing investors, similar as adventure capital enterprises, tapping your 401(k), or adopting from musketeers and family. Each of these options have pitfalls and benefits. For illustration, credit cards will probably have advanced interest rates than regular business loans. Borrowing from musketeers and family risks a particular relationship if your business expansion is n't as economic as you anticipated.

9. Invest in your workers
Growing your business will probably bear bringing on new people. Whether you expand using full- time workers, contractors, or freelancers it's a good idea to have your hiring plan in place and ready to go. This

way, you wo n't be caught off guard if your business grows faster than you anticipate. After all, you would n't want to turn away business or lose your living guests because you ca n't keep up with demand. Taking care of your being staff and letting them know they 're appreciated is also important. A high rate of development among your workers can lead to a loss of effectiveness and quality that could lead to a loss of guests. By offering training to your workers, and openings for growth within your company, you can give your workers an incitement to stay with your business.

10. Consider an expansion of your product or service immolations

Adding new products and services can be a good way to expand your business and increase gains. You might start by looking at your current demand, what guests like about your business, and get their input on any new products, services, or advancements they 'd like to see. You can also look at where your business is most profitable and where you see the topmost demand. Of course, you also need to consider changes in the business and any trends within your assiduity; especially among your challengers. It's also worth considering your area of moxie, and those of your workers. Whenever you expand your product line, you need to make sure you can do so while maintaining the same quality and norms that your guests anticipate.

11. Forge mutually salutary hookups

Your client base offers a chance to grow your business through referrals and hookups. Ask your most satisfied guests to post online reviews and to mention your business to their own musketeers and business mates. A satisfied client who promotes you on social media will probably carry further weight than a paid announcement. It's also free. You could also establish hookups with businesses in fields that frequently cross with your own. For illustration, the fields of real estate, construction, landscaping, drawing services, installation services, and moving companies all relate to each other. They probably have guests who are in colorful stages of home power, or businesses looking to buy and vend property. It would be mutually salutary for these businesses to recommend each other to their guests.

Network

Attending networking events can help you spread the word about your business, meet implicit guests and business leaders in your community. Your original chamber of commerce could be a vital resource for this. You might also look for speaking openings where you or someone on your platoon can partake knowledge about a subject related to your business. Give back to the community Being socially responsible can help you connect with others in your community and spread mindfulness about your business. Financing charity events can also be a good way to dothis.However, it can also spread mindfulness of your business and give people a good print, If you and your platoon levy for charitableevents.However, you might consider hosting a charitable event or help run a fundraiser, If you have the space and coffers. still, it may be wise to invest in special event insurance content to cover your business from any pitfalls that come on with the fresh bottom business on that big day, If you do decide to host your own networking or charity event.

CHAPTER 10

THE JOURNEY AHEAD

Congratulations, adventurer! You've survived storms, turned hurdles into stepping monuments, and now, as we stand at the point of this chapter, it's time to peer toward the horizon of your entrepreneurial trip. In Chapter 10, we'll be your compass, guiding you as you chart the course for the instigative chapters yet to unfold.

Let's start by reflecting on the ground covered. Your small- scale business has evolved, faced challenges, and grown stronger. But the trip is not over; it's just getting started. We will take a moment to celebrate your achievements and admit the assignments learned. suppose of it as a hole stop where you can recharge before the coming leg of your adventure.

Now, let's blink into the unknown – the uncharted homes of the business geography. What lies ahead? New openings, undiscovered requests, and fresh challenges. Together, we'll map how to navigate this unexplored terrain, icing you are well-prepared for the twists and turns that await.

Consider this chapter as a planning session for the chapters to come. We will claw into setting pretensions and creating a roadmap for your business. What mileposts do you want to achieve? What new chops do you want to acquire? It's about visioning the future you want for your business and laying the root to make it a reality.

But we are not just talking strategy; we are also talking about maintaining the spirit of adventure. Your trip should be instigative, not just a series of tasks. We will explore ways to inoculate passion into your work, keeping the honey of alleviation burning brightly as you forge ahead.

The trip ahead is a blank runner staying for your story. Let's fill it with bold opinions, unanticipated discoveries, and the exhilaration of seeing your small- scale business grow into commodity extraordinary. So, snare your pen, adventurer, and let's embark on the coming instigative chapter together!

As we stand on the cusp of a new chapter, fantasize the verbal path of your entrepreneurial trip. This section is not just about looking back; it's about embracing the exhilaration of the unknown that lies ahead. Picture it as a oil staying for your encounter strokes, ready to paint the coming masterpiece of your business adventure. In the rearview glass, you see the challenges conquered and the growth achieved. Now, turn your aspect forward. What awaits? New geographies, unexplored homes, and fresh openings. Together, we'll be your attendants, helping you navigate these uncharted waters with confidence and excitement.

Think of this chapter as a strategic planning session for the future. We will claw into setting bournes and casting a roadmap for your business's coming way. What peaks do you want to peak? What chops do you aim to master? It's about featuring big and laying the foundation for those dreams to materialize.

But this is not just a discussion on business strategy. It's also a memorial to keep the spark alive in your trip. How can you inoculate passion into your work, making every day an adventure rather than a roster? We will explore ways to keep the exhilaration of alleviation burning as you forge ahead into unexplored home.

The trip ahead is a blank oil awaiting your unique strokes. Let's fill it with daring opinions, unanticipated surprises, and the excitement of witnessing your small- scale business evolve into commodity extraordinary. So, snare your favorite pen, let your imagination run wild, and let's embark on the coming exhilarating chapter together!

Reflections and Future Plans for a Continued Prosperous Venture

As we pull over and take a breath, let's do some reflecting. This chapter is like flipping through the runners of a print reader, ignoring about the trip that is brought us right then, right now.

Suppose about the triumphs big and small. What moments made you smile? What challenges tutored you commodity precious? This is further than a hole stop; it's a chance to gather assignments and celebrate the little palms that got you to this point.

Now, let's turn our aspect to the future. Picture it like a blank oil, staying for your coming strokes. We are not just talking strategy then; we are talking dreams and bournes . What do you want for your small-scale business? What peaks are you aiming to climb? Together, let's sketch out a plan that aligns with your dreams, a roadmap for the uninterrupted success of your adventure.

Celebrate the strengths that brought you then and be open about the areas where growth is possible. This is your story, and each chapter is a chance to learn, acclimatize, and grow.

It's not just about sustaining; it's about thriving.

So, snare a mug of your favorite pop, sit back, and let's sputter about your trip. We will explore strategies to make the utmost of what you've learned, attack challenges, and drink the instigative openings staying just around the corner. After all, this is your adventure your story of growth and substance. Let's pick up the pen and write the coming chapters together!

As the seasons change, so too do the requirements of our trials. In the spirit of renewal, let's take a moment to reflect on the vibrant shade of our prosperous adventure and sketch out a roadmap for its continued flourishing.

Looking Back with Gratitude:

Celebrate Triumphs: What mileposts have been reached? What challenges have been overcome? Relive these moments with your platoon, admitting the fidelity and collaborative trouble that fueled the trip.

Check Assignments Learned: Every experience, positive or negative, offers precious perceptivity. dissect strengths and sins, relating areas for enhancement and optimization.

Honor benefactions: Fete the individual benefactions that paved the way for success. Expressing appreciation strengthens bonds and fosters a culture of participated power.

Gaping Ahead with Ambition:
Upgrade your Vision: Has your original vision evolved? Readdress your core values and charge, icing they still guide your path and inspire your platoon. Identify Untapped Implicit: Where do new openings lie? Conduct request exploration, explore arising trends, and communicate innovative ways to expand your reach.
Set Measurable pretensions: Define clear, attainable objects for the coming months and times. These goals must to be time-bound, relevant, quantifiable, achievable, and

targeted (PRAGMATIC). Embrace Innovation In moment's dynamic geography, recession is a form for decline. Encourage creativity, trial, and the disquisition of new technologies and models.

Invest in Your People: Your platoon is your most precious asset. Invest in their professional development, fostering a culture of nonstop literacy and particular growth.

Nurturing Growth

Strengthens hookups: Collaboration can be a important machine for growth. Identify strategic mates who round your strengths and broaden your reach. Foster a Culture of Excellence: Set high norms and cultivate a culture of responsibility and nonstop enhancement. Celebrate successes but also encourage healthy threat- taking and learning from failures.

Prioritize Sustainability: insure your uninterrupted substance thrives alongside environmental and social responsibility. apply sustainable practices and give back to the communities that support you. Flash back, continued substance isn't a sprint; it's a marathon. By regularly reflecting on your trip, nurturing your platoon, and conforming to the evolving geography, you can insure your adventure continues to bloom and leave a lasting heritage of success. So, let's raise a toast to the history, embrace the present, and set our sights on a luminous future.

Your prosperous adventure awaits, ready to blossom into commodity indeed more magnific. May your trials continue to touch lives, enkindle possibilities, and leave the world a little brighter than you set up it.

CHAPTER 11

RESOURCES FOR ONGOING GROWTH

Traditionally, three coffers were considered essential to gormandize growth access to finance, mortal coffers and request access. Or, in simpler terms

Plutocrat

People

Client

As this is primarily a blog about marketing and not finance, I 'm going to talk substantially about the last two of these, but be in no mistrustfulness that the first – access to capital – is abecedarian to business growth. You can not invest in people or pay for marketing to gain guests without the plutocrat. All three are naturally linked; the right people can help you get the finance and deliver the marketing you need to reach guests. Attracting guests helps you with the plutocrat. All three coffers have to be present at the same time for a high- growth strategy.

Getting the right people

While a company might consider its success dependent on invention in core functionality and growth openings in crucial sectors, that's only half the story. " People are our most important resource " isn't just a glib cliché; it's absolutely true. A growth company needs people who can do the job, manage with rapid-fire change, and acclimatize to the evolving organisational terrain. They, thus, need to be creative, flexible and quick learners. They need to have their own vision, but they also need to be suitable to follow the company's vision too. At the operation position, they need to be suitable to lead, work in a platoon, and work on their own when necessary. A growth company needs directors who suppose like entrepreneurs and are n't hysterical to pitch in with everyone differently when circumstances call for it.

From this description, you can guess these people aren't that common. And indeed, a lack of quality key labor force is one of the most limiting factors for a growing company. So, it should go without saying that these people are immensely precious and pivotal to a high- growth plan. This point takes us back to our first resource – plutocrat – without the investment necessary to pay for and retain talented staff, a company will struggle to achieve growth.

Getting guests
Marketing is the business of getting guests. Therefore, your third essential tool for a business success strategy is a strong marketing plan.

Again, plutocrat will be demanded to finance a marketing plan and to hire the right people to conceive and apply it. In the history, the thing for utmost companies aiming for rapid-fire growth would presumably have been to make a bigger deals force. But with the revolution in marketing brought on by changing stations and the Internet, old- academy ways of selling are no longer effective or profitable. You may still need a small salesforce(depending on your product, service or assiduity), but the main thrust should be hiring marketing people and content generators.

Why happy generators?

Well, let's take a nanosecond to look at the ultramodern buying process known as the Buyer's trip. Buyers go on a ' journey ' through three stages mindfulness Stage The buyer realises they've a problem. Consideration Stage The buyer defines their problem and researches options to break it. Decision Stage The buyer chooses a result. Research tells us that the ultramodern buyer will come to you, formerly sure of what they're looking for, having done their exploration. You need to make an impact during the mindfulness and consideration stages and support the decision stage – which requires content and plenitude of it. But it's not a question of volume OR quality

– it has to be both. Creating helpful content applicable to the buyer's stage is the key to B2B inbound marketing. So you need good content generators – pens, editors, videographers, presenters,etc. A good content creation platoon is a critical resource and essential to growth. They will publish content that helps buyers define their problems, probe results and come to a decision – and if they do it right – also your business stands a good chance of being in the handling when the purchase is made. Other critical marketing coffers include a robust system to manage the content, connections, engagement, leads, prospects and transformations. These can each be managed by separate pieces of software from separate merchandisers, but there are real benefits(including time and cost savings) to a decent each- by- one result similar as HubSpot. The marketing platoon can also be supported by a specialist external agency that can help by creating fresh content and furnishing specialist support, training and consultancy. Other important factors moment's requests are ever more competitive and ever more transparent. We know further about our challengers and publish further about ourselves than ever. The Internet has assured universal access to information and coffers for producing products and services. So competitive edge can frequently come down to two simple factors Having a great product/ service Having an morality your buyer can relate to With the ubiquitous sharing of information between peers on social media, review spots and away, it's insolvable to thrive and indeed tougher to survive if your product or service is unacceptable(unless you're a monopoly, of course). And that includes your after- deals service, too. So having a solid product or service is a prerequisite for doing business in moment's marketable geography. But that's only the starting point – you'll need a great product or service to achieve high growth. Because in numerous diligence moment, products and services are veritably unevenly matched, the buying decision can frequently come down to which company the buyer feels further affinity with. As an illustration – consider two companies supplying the exact same specification of product, but the first is a notorious polluter of the terrain and does little for the original community, while the second has taken way to insure they cover the terrain and supports the original community. Given the product is the same specification and does the same job, any nicely acclimated mortal being would buy from the alternate company.

Helpful Tools and References to Support Your Business Endeavors

A Navigation Kit for Aspiring Entrepreneurs Embarking on a business venture can be equal parts exhilarating and daunting. Whether you're a seasoned entrepreneur or a fresh-faced newbie, having the right tools and resources at your disposal can make the journey smoother and more successful.

This guide serves as your navigation kit, packed with helpful tools and references to steer you through various aspects of your business endeavors.

Charting Your Course:

Business Plan Templates: Craft a roadmap for your business with free, customizable templates from organizations like the Small Business Administration (SBA) and SCORE.

Market Research Tools: Gain valuable insights into your target audience and industry with platforms like Google Trends, Similarweb, and Statista.

Financial Management Software: Simplify bookkeeping and financial projections with user-friendly software like QuickBooks, Xero, and FreshBooks.

Building Your Dream Team:

Recruitment Platforms: Find talented individuals to join your team through platforms like LinkedIn, Indeed, and Glassdoor.

Project Management Tools: Keep your team organized and on track with platforms like Asana, Trello, and Monday.com.

Communication Tools: Stay connected with your team and clients through tools like Slack, Zoom, and Microsoft Teams.

Marketing Your Masterpiece:
Social Media Management Tools: Schedule and optimize your social media posts with tools like Hootsuite, Buffer, and Sprout Social.

Email Marketing Platforms: Engage your audience and nurture leads with platforms like Mailchimp, Constant Contact, and ActiveCampaign.

Website Building Platforms: Create a professional website with easy-to-use platforms like Wix, Squarespace, and Shopify.

Learning and Growing:
Online Courses and Webinars: Expand your knowledge base with online courses and webinars from platforms like Coursera, Udemy, and edX.

Business Podcasts and Blogs: Stay up-to-date on industry trends and insights by listening to podcasts and reading blogs from reputable sources.

Industry Publications and Associations: Subscribe to industry publications and join relevant associations to stay connected with the latest developments and network with fellow professionals.

Remember, this is just a starting point.
The vast ecosystem of tools and resources available can feel overwhelming, but the key

is to identify what best suits your specific needs and business goals. Don't hesitate to experiment, adapt, and refine your toolkit as your venture evolves. With the right tools and references in your arsenal, you'll be well-equipped to navigate the exciting and challenging world of business, turning your entrepreneurial dreams into tangible realities.

Bonus Tip: Utilize government resources and support programs specifically designed to assist small businesses. The SBA, for example, offers a wealth of free resources, workshops, and funding opportunities.

So, chart your course, build your team, market your masterpiece, and never stop learning and growing. With the right tools and a determined spirit, you can navigate the journey towards a successful and fulfilling business venture.

CONCLUSION

As we close the pages of this book, take a moment to reflect on the incredible journey we've shared. Your small-scale business has evolved, faced challenges head-on, and grown stronger. In this concluding chapter, let's celebrate your achievements and cast a hopeful gaze toward the vibrant future that awaits.

We began by laying the foundation, understanding the essence of entrepreneurship, and crafting a vision for your business. Along the way, we faced storms, turned hurdles into stepping stones, and navigated the uncharted waters of the business landscape. Each chapter was a step in your unique entrepreneurial story—a story filled with resilience, innovation, and a passion for growth.

Now, let's raise a toast to your achievements, both big and small. Whether it was conquering a challenging market, expanding your customer base, or simply learning something new, every triumph is a testament to your dedication and hard work. Take pride in these moments; they are the building blocks of your success.

As we look toward the future, envision your business as a canvas waiting for the next strokes. The roadmap we've crafted together is a guide, not a rigid plan. It's a compass to navigate the exciting opportunities that lie ahead. Embrace the unknown with optimism, knowing that each challenge is a chance to learn and each new chapter is an opportunity to grow.

This isn't just a conclusion; it's a commencement—a commencement of a new phase in your entrepreneurial journey. So, take a deep breath, savor the sense of accomplishment, and get ready to script the next chapters of your small-scale business venture.

Thank you for being a part of this journey. May your future be bright, your ambitions boundless, and your entrepreneurial spirit unwavering.

REVIEW

Your Feedback Matters

Hi Reader,

I hope this message finds you well. As someone valued in our community, I wanted to reach out and personally ask for your feedback.

Your experience with Starting small-scale business
is important to us, and we genuinely value the opinions of our customers. Whether

you've recently made a purchase, utilized our services, or engaged with our content, your insights can make a significant impact.

Would you be willing to take a few moments to share your thoughts with us? Your feedback not only helps us understand what we're doing right but also provides valuable insights into areas where we can improve.

You can leave a review on [Platform of Choice] or respond to this email with your thoughts. We are constantly striving to enhance our offerings, and your input plays a crucial role in this process.

Thank you so much for your time and consideration. We genuinely appreciate your support.

Best Regards,

Arnette C. Briggs